THE HEART OF THE
Wedding

"Gerry Fierst has written an exciting, valuable book that addresses part of the confusion we have over marriage. His journey with couples restores the beauty and transformational aspects of marriage ceremony. He plucked the marriage event from its ordinary place of being only public declaration and sharing of taxes and insurance to reveal the power of transformation that draws two people into a circle of love. Poets like Neruda, Tagore and Barrett Browning remind us of the legacy of love language we have as a world culture. Fierst's deep and meaningful work as a Storyteller and Actor/Director of Theatre combine with his growing wisdom to help couples find their unique story to symbolize the Marriage Day. They add their own spice and flavoring but still draw upon the best of time honored parts of the ritual. His cross-cultural and cross-gender perspectives leave a bread crumb trail to show how marriage as a ceremony is meant to be inclusive, open to all. I love *The Heart of the Wedding* and would recommend it to anyone but it would be a drink of cool water in the desert to someone contemplating getting married."

— ELAINE WYNNE, M.A., Licensed Psychologist and Storyteller Contributor to "BETWIXT AND BETWEEN, Patterns of Masculine and Feminine Initiation," L. Mahdi, Ed., Open Court

"*The Heart of the Wedding* reconnects the marriage ritual to our twenty-first century lives. Gerald Fierst, celebrant, poet, and storyteller, fills chapter after chapter with examples of ceremonies showing that weddings need not be Victorian relics, but can be filled with a sense of fun and adventure, as well as common sense. Acknowledging our multi-cultural nation where people of every race, faith, and heritage meet and marry, this book celebrates the new America, respecting tradition while finding a contemporary voice to say 'I do.' Gerry brings to this book the same care, precision and artistry I have seen him bring to all of his projects. By connecting life's passages with a larger vision of humanity — past, present and future — Gerry shows us a way to celebrate our families and ourselves."

— SUSAN O'HALLORAN, Director, RaceBridges, Chicago, Illinois

THE HEART OF THE

Wedding
GERALD FIERST

Parkhurst Brothers, Inc., Publishers

LITTLE ROCK

Our National Conversation
Raising the level of public discourse

www.pbros.net

Parkhurst Brothers books are distributed to the trade through the Chicago Distribution Center, a unit of the University of Chicago Press, and may be ordered through Ingram Book Company, Baker & Taylor, Follett Library Resources and other book industry wholesalers. To order from the University of Chicago's Chicago Distribution Center, phone 1-800-621-2736 or send a fax to 1-800-621-8476. Copies of this and other Parkhurst Brothers, Inc., Publishers titles are available to organizations and corporations for purchase in quantity by contacting Special Sales Department at our home office location, listed on our website.

Printed in Canada

First Edition 2011

2010 2011 2012 2013 2014 2015 2016 2017 2018   18 17 16 15 14 13 12 11 10 9 8 7 6 5 4 3 2 1

Library of Congress Control Number: 2009942596

ISBN: Original Trade Paperback: 978-1-935166-22-1 [10 digit: 1-935166-22-0]

This book is printed on archival-quality paper that meets requirements of the American National Standard for Information Sciences, Permanence of Paper, Printed Library Materials, ANSI Z39.48-1984.

Design Director and Dustjacket/cover design:
Wendell E. Hall

Page design:
Shelly Culbertson

Acquired for Parkhurst Brothers, Inc., Publishers by:
Ted Parkhurst

Editor:
Roger Armbrust

Proofreaders:
Bill and Barbara Paddack

TABLE of CONTENTS

9 FOREWORD
THE HEART of THE WEDDING:
HOW to SAY I DO
CELEBRATING a NEW BEGINNING

13 CHAPTER ONE
HAPPILY EVER ONWARD

26 CHAPTER TWO
UNDERSTANDING RITUAL
AND THE SPIRITUAL

40 CHAPTER THREE
A HISTORY of WEDDING:
COMING DOWN THE AISLE
ALL DRESSED IN WHITE

60 CHAPTER FOUR
TEN TIPS FOR WEDDING

76 CHAPTER FIVE
DEALING WITH FAMILY

88 CHAPTER SIX
PARTNERSHIP – THREE COUPLES'
HEART OF WEDDING

101 CHAPTER SEVEN
RECOMMITMENT CEREMONIES:
MAKING THE OLD WORDS NEW
HOW DO I LOVE THEE?
LET ME COUNT THE WAYS.

127 CHAPTER EIGHT
WHAT IS A MARRIAGE?

136 CHAPTER NINE
BLASTS — THE BEST WEDDINGS

147 CHAPTER TEN
DOING IT FOR YOURSELF

169 CHAPTER ELEVEN
NEW AND OLD BLESSINGS

184 CHAPTER TWELVE
LEGALLY EVER AFTER

201 INDEX

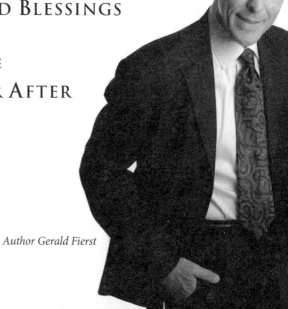

Author Gerald Fierst

THE HEART OF THE WEDDING: HOW TO SAY I DO

CELEBRATING A NEW BEGINNING

A wedding ceremony is a crossroad where two life stories intersect.

A wedding ceremony takes the two lives that the individuals have traveled and transforms them into a single path upon which each life embarks, starting over.

A wedding ceremony acknowledges the turning point, the choice to go on. It's the setting off on life's journey together, with the experiences of the past as a guide into the future.

A wedding ceremony is a story which tells the past, proclaims the present, and blesses the future.

There is a folktale about a bride whose betrothed lover returns from war depressed and aloof. She despairs that they will ever be able to start their lives again. At last, she seeks the help of a wise old woman. "One must go and pluck a tiger's whisker to discover how to heal a heart," says the crone.

So night after night, the desperate bride goes into the jungle seeking the tiger. Eventually, she finds the trail, follows the tracks, and discovers the lair. She smells the beast; hears its roar. She stands frozen with fear as the tiger passes near. Eventually, she dares to step closer to the tiger's cave. In this way, night by night, step by step, she approaches the monster that might devour her.

Finally, she begins to leave offerings of food for the tiger. Then, one night, the tiger emerges from his cave, and, as she stands frozen, heart beating, he approaches her, sits before her, and patiently waits for his meat. The woman places the bowl which she has brought in front of the tiger, and as he eats, she reaches forth and plucks a whisker. Then, she runs hard and fast to the aged crone.

"Make your magic," the woman says. The old lady looks at her in astonishment. "You have already made the magic. Patience has made the impossible become real. Now, you must trust patience to make reality become possible."

The bride returned home to marry her betrothed, and, with patience, she healed his wounded soul, and they started over.

Words have power. Stories change us. The old stories are landscapes of the human psyche in which every turn is a comment on the human life journey, and every action is a marking of universal needs and a recording of universal emotions. We are all wounded and shell-shocked by growing up. We all despair of healing. We all face the beast and, in mad desperation, do what we would never sensibly do — plucking the whisker and running for our lives. We just all do it in different ways. If we are lucky, there is a wise crone or a friendly magician who tells us that we already have the power to leave regret behind and start again.

In our post industrial era, we do not put great store in the magical power of symbols and the psychic patterning of images. In the 21st Century, popular culture sees stories as a realistic reflection of, or an ironic commentary on, factual events. Only religion tries to maintain living story, offering prayers and blessings with the power to move us forward on our spiritual and life journey. Yet, even there, fundamentalist movements try to enchain the mythic with literal interpretation — to the impoverishment of us all. The result is the diminishing of ritual ceremonies into decorations for life passages, rather than truly empowering experiences of vital change. For this reason, many couples, considering ritual as empty words, give short shrift to the wedding's ceremonial aspects and, instead, concentrate on the consumer values of presents and parties; but we shouldn't throw the baby out with the bath water. Neither faith nor dogma is necessary for magic, and a wedding ceremony should be magic. Traditional ritual structure followed the alchemical formula for change and renewal; so today, meaningful secular ritual can be created with the power of ancient formulas by layering personal and traditional story. The ancient patterns of ritual are all based on story formulas which energize the life force, giving us the insight and wisdom to proceed through life's course. In our life ceremonies, we tell our personal story, and we retell the great story of all creation — birth, life, death, and rebirth. By marking our passages, ritual connects us to the mythic, to each other, to past, to present, and to future.

In 1973, Lionel Murphy, the visionary attorney general of Australia, understood this need for secular ritual. He was a divorced Catholic, and when he wanted to remarry, he found that getting a civil ceremony was not too different from getting a dog license. He felt that everyone should have the opportunity to celebrate their life events with words that reflect their passions, joys, hopes, and traditions. Therefore, he created the concept of a civil celebrant, an officiant who would write and perform ceremonies as special as the lives being celebrated. Today, celebrants perform the majority of weddings in Australia — as well as baby namings, coming-of-age ceremonies, and funerals.

In 2001, philanthropists Pat and Gaile Sarma founded The Celebrant USA Foundation & Institute in Montclair, New Jersey, bringing the concept to the United States. The foundation now offers an extensive curricula in life-passage ceremonies leading to North American certification as a civil celebrant. A celebrant is a director, co-creator, writer, and guide. Ceremonies are developed through an interview process during which clients define their needs and tastes. While one could write one's own ceremony, a celebrant is the crone who helps clients recognize the power in their own story — the power of past moving into future. In a time when many couples come from vastly different cultural and religious traditions and do not have access to or reject religious ritual, the celebrant puts the magic back into the ceremony, connecting it to the milestone life event it truly incorporates.

As in Australia, weddings represent the largest market for celebrants in the U.S. In America, the average wedding costs $25,000. Food, drink, flowers and costumes are given lavish attention. What of the ceremony? What of the words that will be spoken? What of the magical formula that renews and transforms? In general, the ceremony receives the least attention of any details of the wedding party; but the ceremony is the heart of the wedding. Happily, more and more couples are defeating the idea that wedding guests are half-listening to the ceremony while hoping for the party to begin soon. In an increasingly multicultural nation, one with growing interest in personal story, wedding couples want to say words that are meaningful and uniquely their own, reflecting their life stories and traditions. Thus, American celebrants are reinvigorating the words of marriage. Bride, groom, family and guests will listen and experience the transformative moment that has called them all together and which sends the hopeful couple onto the path of life.

I am one of the first American Civil Celebrants, trained in 2002 by Dally Messenger III who was one of Australia's first civil celebrants and founder and principal of the International College of Celebrancy in Melbourne, Australia. I gained my Diploma of Marriage Celebrancy from the International College and was later certified by the North American Celebrant Foundation. Dally took Lionel Murphy's ideas and brought them into reality. He instilled in me a deep respect for the importance of marking our lives with ceremony. As a storyteller and theater artist, I already understood the powerful effect of layering a ceremony's words with images, narrative, rhythms and movement. Studying for certification, I compared the parallel patterns of ceremonies around the world. As I began to write ceremonies for American couples, I added my training as an actor to ground these ceremonial templates in the reality of our lives as 21st Century Americans. An actor's first training is to be present in the moment and to use the power of reality to animate the story being told. The stories I hear and retell within wedding ceremonies are filled with laughter and heartbreak, dramatic events, and the ordinary pleasures of our shared lives. They reflect who we are now and who we are becoming as individuals and as a nation. I look forward to hearing them as I continue to write ceremonies and officiate at weddings. I believe that in the next decades, civil celebrants will come to perform the majority of weddings in America. This book is one step towards that goal and to the goal of restoring ceremony as the Heart of Wedding.

I particularly want to thank my friends Ellen Blaney, Helen Kagan, and Judy Trotter who read these chapters as they were being written, offering invaluable suggestions and encouragement. I also want to thank Dally and Remi Messenger, who set me on my course as a civil celebrant. I'm very grateful also to the wonderful couples who gladly permitted me to use their stories and ceremonies. Thank you, Alice and Hazel, Ben and Amelia, Chris and Leah, Richard and Alexandra Augustyn, PJ and Sandy Benedetti, Michelle and Todd Carlstrom, John and Lee Chow, Ed and Maki Cleveland, Scott Clugstone and Wallace Norman, Christopher and Alysha Day, David and Chei Frank, Eric Fritts and Lisa Jenkinson, Terence and Anjalee Galion, Stephanie Goloway and Michael Hospodar, Edward Gormley and Pamela Eng, Daniel Masler and Kristina Hagman, Ronald and Rosemarie Matthews, William and Keri Mendrzycki, John and Gretchen Oury, Jim and Joni Porter, Edward and Norlyn Poto, Alyson and Jose Rodriquez, Mark and Nancy Rogerson, Pearl Sloane, Jeffrey Smith and Tammy Probst, Angelo and Donna Testa, Greg and Sabrina Tiesi, Mike Whipple and Julia John-Whipple. One of the pleasures of writing this book was speaking to all of you again, hearing how your family and friends still talk about the warmth and intimacy of your ceremony, and finding you all well and still married! I want to thank my editor Roger Armbrust for making me into a much better writer and Ted Parkhurst for his support of this book. Finally, I want to thank my wife Marjorie and my granddaughter Anjel for encouragement and endurance while I took over the kitchen table.

Chapter One

HAPPILY EVER ONWARD

Why do we choose to marry? Why have wedding ceremonies? How do our wedding vows affect us?

I have asked these questions to couples old and young. Some of these individuals have married for the second and third time. Everyone I questioned looked at me with incredulity. Of course, they wanted to get married, even though at times they had sworn they never would do so; but having met the one they love, they feel that marriage is an obvious choice. Their relationship had reached a critical mass, and they now needed and wanted to have a public voice of commitment.

A wedding ceremony should portray a couple's evolving relationship — a layering of images that reveals one's past, celebrates the present, and emphasizes one's hopes for the future.

Let me introduce you to six real couples who intend to make a life together. Their varieties of ceremonies express the values and love which brought them together, and upon which they intend to build their futures. Following these brief introductions, you'll receive more detailed views into each couple's story.

Practice Towards Perfect

My friends Kristina and Daniel were married at a Zen center in Jemez Springs, New Mexico.

A Buddhist priest banged a drum rhythmically while the couple recited the traditional Zen Buddhist Heart Sutra. Then Hosen, a Buddhist nun in beautiful, grey silk robes, asked questions like: "Will you refrain from sleeping with other people?" When Daniel or Kristina said yes, Hosen would bang two pieces of wood together loudly, responding in a loud voice, "GOOD!"

"If you fight, will you talk to each other and try to work it out?"..."Yes."..."GOOD!"

All the while a second priest was gently banging the drum.

At some point, Kaya — Daniel and Kristina's two-year-old daughter who had crawled out of a friend's arms — started banging the drum, too.

"Will you think of what is best for the other person and watch out for them?"... "Yes."..."GOOD!"

"Will you refrain from hurting this person in deed or in word?"..."Yes."..."GOOD!"

After Kristina and Daniel offered each other a cup of sake, they went outside together into the light snow and banged a big gong.

That was fifteen years ago. Kaya will soon go off to college.

Luck and Work

Lisa and Eric were married in a beautiful, vaulted church. The setting seemed traditional, but the bride wore a scarlet gown. As a couple, Eric identifies himself as the dreamer and adventurer, while Lisa thinks she's more practical and traditional. Lisa and Eric wanted a civil ceremony, but they also wanted their wedding to have the sense of beauty and tradition which ritual instills. They chose me to be their officiant because they knew my reputation as a storyteller, and they asked me to read a poem. They wanted their ceremony to reflect the eccentric journey of their 13-year courtship. Soon after their wedding, Eric received an offer to transfer from New Jersey to Southern California. He had always wanted to live in that area of the country, and now the opportunity had arrived. Lisa gave up her long-time job in New Jersey and found a new job in California. So, they moved from the east to the west. A year after their move, both of them have been laid off. Now they are trying to plan their future together. Rather than wondering at their bad luck, they realize how fortunate they are to have each other.

Renewed Possibilities

Norlyn's first husband committed suicide. She was widowed for 10 years before she married Ed. When they met, Ed was recovering from a painful divorce. Their wedding was a joyful celebration of renewed possibility. The bride came down the aisle to the rock-musical strains of "Girls Just Want to Have Fun." Three years later, Ed is retired. He gets up every morning to see his wife off to work. Norlyn thinks of herself as the Queen of Joy, married to her best friend, and able to imagine the rest of their lives together as an ever-expanding experience of happiness. They have made the decision that life is only lived once, and, with comfortable financial resources, they plan to fulfill their dreams, sharing their adventures and life together with their family and friends.

Future Dreams

Ed and Maki met as students getting their degrees in hotel-and-food management. They married the week they graduated. Their wedding used the backdrop of New York City, celebrating the style and excitement of the life they plan to build together. Maki now works for a high-end Manhattan florist doing floral arrangements, and

Ed manages a hotel for a major New York hospital. Eventually they would like to be partners at work as well as at home. Their ambition is to start a party-planning and catering business of their own.

This Moment Together

Both Nancy and Mark had failed marriages before they met each other. Nancy had children. She swore she would never marry again. Marc had to pass the test. It wasn't easy. Family dynamics had to change. Old wounds had to heal. Mark says, "Some people speak of a relationship as a tug of war. It's not; it's a give and take. Relationships don't make a circle; they make a figure eight. Two individuals meet at a common point where you find your happy place." Mark and Nancy see their future enriched by each other's love and support. Their marriage ceremony celebrated the new life they would build together.

A Hidden Treasure

Stephanie and Michael had met in college and remained good friends after they each married other partners and had children. Their families played together. After Stephanie divorced her first husband, she moved to the other side of the state, and she and Michael lost touch; but when Stephanie divorced her second husband, Michael had also divorced his wife. In the midst of their lives' parallel upheaval, Stephanie reconnected with Michael's former wife, who suggested that Stephanie ought to call Michael, too. "He could use a friend." Stephanie and Michael had been friends for 35 years and reconnected immediately. At their wedding, they broke open a geode as a symbol of the treasure hidden before our eyes, and only found when life breaks us apart.

Michael says, "My first wife left me. I was kicked to the curb. I didn't connect to anyone, and then I met Stephanie again. I just loved her. It wasn't a big jump to begin planning a life." Stephanie says, "You just go with your guts and intuition." They were married on their porch. They hope to retire soon and build a community of "green geezers" based on environmental and social activism.

A Threshold into the Future

Each of these couples speaks of their marriage ceremony as a threshold; not a beginning, but a stile or passage over which they crossed in order to transform. A wedding is not only a couple's public announcement of their intention to make a life together, but also, by their witnessing, a contract that henceforth the community will recognize the couple as a family. The nuance of family versus couple is important. A family is bound by ties that cannot be broken. We are forever connected to our parents and siblings by the facts of biology. The wedding ceremony creates such a bond with faith — not religious faith, although that certainly is used by some as glue — but the universal, human faith in future possibilities. After I communicated with Ed and Maki about their wedding and marriage, Ed wrote to me, "I guess in marriage at times some things are understood but unspoken. But then when you actually speak about it, you say to yourself, 'Why haven't we ever really talked this out before?' I believe we both became a little more focused on what we want to accomplish in life."

A wedding ceremony is the beginning of the conversation among you, your spouse, and the community about the future. The ceremony completes a journey and opens the way to new directions.

If Lisa and Eric had not been married, Lisa wonders whether they would have stayed together. "He would have gone to California and I would have stayed back east. Life doesn't always bring the path we plan. Saying the words out loud in front of people made it harder to ignore them."

The Power of Words

Too often, our culture forgets that words possess power far beyond their literal meaning. One can say "I love you" privately and experience the words' full force in the moment; but ritual frames the words within past, present, and future, giving the personal a context and weight that opens us to responsibility and maturity.

When Stephanie and Michael were married, Stephanie wrote a parable about a maiden who felt that she could jump off a bridge without forethought:

> She climbed up the bank and stood on the bridge. Remembering times in her youth when she and her cousins made sport of jumping from cliffs, she took a deep breath and leapt into the darkness. What an exhilarating thrill!!!!!! Proud that she had followed the men, she swam across the lake, expecting cheers of celebration.
>
> Instead, a tall, handsome Viking warrior came up to her and fiercely said: "What? Are you bezerkers? Jumping off a bridge like that is not wise, fair princess. Do you even know how deep the water is? Do you have any idea what kinds of logs and branches might be lurking from the bottom of the lake? Jumping off a bridge, into unknown waters, when you are cold and tired from merriment...not safe... not safe..."
>
> The princess's women friends looked on aghast, for it was well-known that the princess did NOT like to be corrected. She flicked her long braids, and they prepared for a storm worthy of Thor.
>
> But then the princess looked into the Viking's eyes. She saw care, and concern, and compassion...such as she had never seen except in the kind, worried eyes of her own dear father. And so she nodded, and thanked the warrior, and agreed that she would not jump off the bridge again.

Their wedding guests already knew the facts of Stephanie and Michael's lives. Everyone knew that each of them had been careless and impetuous in their previous years, jumping with passion instead of caution; but now the time had come to look into each other's eyes and recognize that love has depths that go beyond grand gestures. The words of this story — said out loud in public — became a transitional formula acknowledging the maturity that would be brought to this new marriage relationship.

A good ceremony forms a magic spell, capturing one's attention and senses, revealing a world of heightened awareness and experience, just as a good play or movie transports us into a different world where time stands still. Our scientific culture dismisses magic because it cannot change the physical world; but magic does present emotional clarity to the psyche. Great poets, orators, and preachers know the magic of the rhythms and images they create. Thus, ceremonial structures exist in every culture. They punctuate our lives at the beginning and end of every new phase and allow us to express our strongest emotions of joy and sadness. As a magician draws a spellbinding circle in which the formula's power intensifies and takes effect, so the wedding officiant makes the circle, transforming the couple by using readings, blessings and stories. These heighten and reveal the psychic transitions taking place within a life passage and meld them within the awareness of the couple and their guests. Words not only acknowledge our present condition, but, in fact, form the tools with which we shape the psyche into a new identity.

"Our ceremony was the merging of all the different aspects of our lives," says Stephanie. "My first two marriages, I was looking for the ideal of a fairytale. Our ministers followed the traditional service. With Mike, the words were my own voice. I can't imagine being more committed."

From Me and Her to We

When Mark and Nancy got married, Mark characterized the moment. "It goes from a *me* and a *her* to a *we* thing. It's the beginning to an end. We lived together first for a little over two years. I don't think you see it before. You see it after. You suddenly realize you have a responsibility. Before — if you are not married — you can always just go. Where afterwards, it's more. Everyone sees it — that you're married. I think it's important. We talked about getting married because we did have kids. They take it a lot more seriously. They recognize that they have to work on being a family with us. But now I know, if we didn't have kids, we would have gotten married anyway. It shows that you are ultimately committed. You're in it to win it. Two people in a row boat, you have to adjust to each other's habits and quirks, because you can't move out of it."

Nancy added that children were important to her decision to remarry, but as they have grown and gone to college, she feels how much the decision to marry was a long-term choice to be with Mark. "The kids see more stability with us. My daughter was crying at the wedding because she was sad. She would have liked it to be just her and me, but she wanted it for me because she wanted me to be happy. She sees that we do things together and for each other. We take the kids out, or I'll make dinner, or he'll make dinner. They see a sense of unity. They see two people who share as opposed to cohabitate.

"Still," Nancy continued, "since we got married, there have been a lot of milestones. My son went to college. My daughter's in college. Now that they're gone, it's a different dynamic. Without them home, it's very different. You begin to appreciate each other a little bit more. When he works nights, it's four days apart. The first two days is fine, but by the second two, I'm beginning to think I've had enough of this. Companionship is the word that I'm looking for."

Nancy and Mark recognize their marriage is a long-term opportunity for adventure and change. Nancy says, "We challenge each other. I take more risks now. I feel more comfortable. I wanted to have that experience with him. This is worth it. We challenge each other in everything, whether it's traveling, home things, cooking. Marriage isn't just adapting to each other's quirks. It's trying on a new role and discovering resources in oneself that are supported and complemented by one's partner."

Her Life is Filled with Joy

Norlyn and Ed also felt that the concern for children was central to their desire to marry. Ed says, "Procreation is important. For the young, it's a custom. Something that's been done through the ages. Marriage gives the format to it. When you're young, you want to have kids. It's the main drive there. These are very strong customs. I had a very hard time with my divorce. It's not something that is done. It's your marriage. You make it work, and you stay together. Divorce is hard for kids. Divorce puts a lot of strain on the people who are closest to you. In the old tradition, you just made it work. But you always have a situation where someone is so self-centered, and after that you go through a divorce, and you lose trust. You don't want to go through that again."

Norlyn and Ed both felt the tension of a failed marriage, and its resulting emotional wounds, versus their desire to have the family structure which they saw as the core of their identities. The idea of trust became the primary definition of why they would remarry.

"It's hard to deal with any person when there is a wall and you cannot pass that wall," Ed explains. "You have no idea what's behind it. The problem there is you cannot trust. How do you trust the person? You do the right thing. Your right thing is not the same as my right thing, but that's how you develop the trust. When you do the right thing, you're depositing into the account; and when you do the wrong thing, you're withdrawing from the account. If you withdraw too many times, the relationship goes bad. If you do this right thing, it eventually works."

Ed notes that sometimes knowing the right thing is not easy. Norlyn and Ed have used their strong sense of family and daily rituals to define the term. "Family is a defining structure for marriage — family ritual and structures. Our kids know what we stand for and what's important to us. Rituals are huge. They make the bonds in family. It makes it possible to look forward to the next time." Norlyn and Ed make ritual out of the conscious decision to see each other off in the morning, to send each other notes, to greet each other at the door at the end of the day. For the family, even though the children are now college age and beyond, traditional holiday and birthday celebrations, as well as special occasions which have become regular events (like June picnics), provide ritual times to note the importance placed on each member within the family. "We work as a family. Our marriage would work without it, but why not have everything if you can. "

Norlyn and Ed included rituals in their wedding ceremony which would connect their children to each other. The children were all asked to light candles and sign a wedding document that stated Ed and Norlyn's promises to each other and to them. When asked what has changed in her life since being married, Norlyn without hesitation says, "I had two daughters and now I have four."

Norlyn and Ed believe in the power of words and images. They understand that by doing and saying — following the patterns of ritual — our lives are shaped and eventually transformed. Their marriage is not only filled with daily rituals to support each other, but also a ritual structure symbolized by their avocation of ballroom dancing, in which each of them is more because of the other. Shortly after they met, she and Ed went to a Viennese ball held at the Waldorf Astoria.

"I was the queen, and he totally embraced me and accepted that I was. Here I was in this magical ball room, with this incredible, handsome man, dancing this magical waltz, and people came up to say we were the most beautiful couple there; and I totally embraced that…Every day is a fountain. You can be more than just a wife and mother and career woman. You can have a truly amazing fantasy and be empowered by that. What a glorious life we have."

When I asked them what advice they would give to others, they replied, "Do the right thing, and have fun, and have as many people as are important to you to come along on the journey." They see the energy which they derive from their marriage as an expansive opportunity to embrace all the people they love. That, in turn, reenergizes their connection as a couple.

Norlyn says, "I'll share with anyone who wants to be in that space with me. If you can engage others in what you believe in, it becomes reality." Norlyn has a box of rhinestone pins shaped like queens' crowns. She gives them away to her friends and family and acquaintances. Each gift is a ritual gesture that offers the other person a chance to be special, a queen. Each gift is a reminder to Norlyn that with Ed, she is the queen, and her life is filled with joy.

Watch Us Grow

Ed and Maki juggled the rituals of different cultures as they planned their wedding. Maki is Japanese. There were rituals of gift-giving. Special teddy bears, weighing the same as the bride's and the groom's birth weight, had to be brought from Japan to give to the bride's and groom's mothers. Family and friends from Japan were coming to New York City for the first, and, perhaps, only time in their lives. The city itself was part of the occasion's excitement and had to be included. Not only were Maki and Ed getting married that week, but they were also graduating from hotel school.

Ed remembers, "The whole ceremony really wasn't for us. It was for everybody else; and all the planning that we did was more focused on making sure that everyone else had a good time. We had her family and friends coming from the other side of the world. For the first time, everybody was in the same place at the same time. We made sure it was an experience for everyone attending."

The ceremony was celebrated at a restaurant with a spectacular view across the East River to the United Nations. A boat tour down the East River followed the wedding dinner. "We wanted it to be an experience," Maki explains. "Our wedding would be their time to see the night views and eat great food. It was the one shot."

The Japanese tradition of gift-giving and honoring the guests emphasized the connection that Ed and Maki felt for the family and friends they were inviting. Maki says, "Without a doubt, we considered every detail, even the way we prepared the favors for the wedding: We bought these little plants. Plant these trees; let them grow. Watch us grow. And we made sure we wrapped them up gorgeously. We bought bottles of wine and decorated them with sparkles. It was for everyone to be included. I went to his mother and to my mother just to hear what they thought. Here in the United States, the wedding says you're celebrating us. We wanted to celebrate everyone."

Ed and Maki found that their effort to include everyone was an expansive experience, focusing and strengthening their extended ties to family and friends. They eventually want to have their own party-planning business. While most of us would be daunted at doing the kind of planning and personal attention they put into their wedding party, they saw it as an opportunity to display their personal style. Their celebration said to each of their guests that this day was not about the couple, but about the family and friends who had come to share.

Maki says, "I enjoyed thinking about what makes people feel good. You get emotionally involved with it. Think about their faces when they see what you have planned. I don't need to be the center of the party."

Maki and Ed's attitude resonates with the weddings of the 19th Century when one would have received family and neighbors into the front parlor. In fact, Ed admits, "Even though it wasn't in our house, it was our thing. If we had a house that was big enough and a yard that was big enough, we might have done it at home." For Ed and Maki, the cultural and practical details of having family coming from Japan made them realize the ceremony and party's ritual expression as a communal celebration, not a personal glorification. "It's like when a rock band applauds the audience for coming to the show," Ed said. "The audience isn't playing, but they're part of the show. You could just buy the album, but it's not the same. The emotion of the fans really helps.

"I was more excited that day because of our planning — to see how all these things we had planned would come off. Because Maki had her hands on it, we were more invested in it. Handmade invitations, searching out the right envelope, the right insert. A lot of people don't give themselves the pleasure. I think for most of the people there who knew us well, we kind of got the feeling they felt, 'That's what we thought we would get from Ed and Maki.' Our first dance was *Can You Feel the Love Tonight*. We had the deejay do a crazy mix, and we broke out in crazy dancing. We did a chicken dance. Everyone thought, 'That's so you. That's so Ed and Maki. We figured you would do something.' The evening confirmed what they already thought of us."

Ed and Maki found that their focus on being hosts strengthened their experience of becoming husband and wife. Embracing their joint effort in creating this large event, with its repeated symbolic expression of their connection to their community, provided an emotional transition into their new identities.

Ed says, "After we cleaned up and everyone was gone, we still got up and went to work, but when we went out it was Mr. and Mrs., and when we went to our families, or when we went to Japan, everyone would look and say, 'This is the man Maki married.' I wouldn't have done it any other way. Obviously you love the person you're with, but if you are going to do it, do it! Going to Las Vegas — what's the point? The day should be a little more important than getting married by Elvis. It should be done as an important occasion even if you go to the courthouse. You don't go in your jeans. You dress up. You do it like you mean it. I think seeing how we did it may open our friends' minds to doing something a little bit different."

When Ed and Maki consider the future together in business or in life, they now recognize the difference between being partners and being husband and wife. Maki says, "The fact that we're married makes us a lot more invested. It's our thing. It's an emotional recognition. I think we're more likely to come to decisions we're happy with. We're going to see each other at the dinner table every night. We don't have a tie breaker if it is just us. As a woman, if you are partners, and the guy decides to move somewhere, you have a choice to leave him or to stay; but you have to make a choice. But in husband and wife, you have to talk about it and decide it together. In business or in marriage, he completes me. I'm comfortable with him when I need something; he has it. It's back and forth — not always that we agree, and it may not be easy for us either — but it is a completing. We know our strengths and our expertise. When we disagree and need to decide, I think if that's where your strength comes from, I will take that leap of faith."

Deeper than 'In Love'

Lisa and Eric needed to take a leap of faith. They had known each other for 13 years. In the beginning, Lisa, 23, had managed a shop in the mall. She had hired Eric, 16, as a clerk. They became the best of friends, but he was a kid. He wanted to go off on adventures. He wanted to follow the Grateful Dead. As he went into his 20s, he pressed Lisa to become more than his best friend. Lisa had never thought the time was right. She was waiting for Eric to grow up. At last, her mother told her, "If you love him, you must go to him." Lisa explains it: "There was a practicality to it. We had broken up and gotten back together so many times. Then we were happy. So I thought this is it." They committed with the traditional vows for better, for worse, for richer, for poorer. Lisa did wear a red gown; perhaps that choice is evidence that not only Eric had a daring side to his personality.

After they were married, Eric's employer wanted him to transfer to southern California. Eric saw it as a "chance and a sign." He had always wanted to move to California. Lisa was less enthusiastic, but it had always been his dream. She gave up a good job and moved. Lisa says, "Getting married was easy. Marriage wasn't a challenge. Our first big challenge was moving." Lisa notes that if they hadn't been married, they might not have stayed together. Eric would have gone with his job, and she would have stayed with hers. But having promised to make their lives together, the job offer became an immediate test.

At their wedding, Lisa and Eric had used the *Owl and the Pussycat* as a reading. It was a prescient choice. Now they were off on an adventure, and they would face challenges. Lisa couldn't find a new job, and Eric was downsized. Their old support system of friends and family was 3,000 miles away.

Once again, if they hadn't been married, they might have broken up; but they *were* married! They had said their vows before family and friends. As Eric bluntly puts it, "A ceremony is a promise, plain and simple. You either break the promise or you keep it." Marriage hadn't changed the problems that had come up between Eric and Lisa over 13 years, but the vows of their marriage ceremony had broken old patterns. "When we married," says Eric, "I didn't know who I was. Living out here, I became different. I started to take a different look at our relationship. Now, we had to actually work on it."

Lisa continued, "All the time that we have invested in each other. Sometimes I felt like a fool that we had done it, but then I took comfort in all the time we did invest. I could think about all the people who are divorced. They don't have what we have. All the time we spent growing up together. Our relationship is deeper than 'in love'." Their new married life in California started to strengthen the connection between Eric and Lisa as they began to develop a network of friends that weren't his or hers, but theirs. Lisa started to experience the outdoor activities that Eric enjoyed. "Suddenly, we had the opportunity," Eric said, "for both of us as a couple to interact as a couple, to move as a unit as opposed to separate." The life passage of marriage hadn't changed them, but expanded them. "Something that was, still is."

The words they had said "for better, for worse" changed the way they perceived themselves and their choices. "We knew we were starting out on a voyage. We hoped for smooth sailing," Lisa noted. "Now I remember a quote I saw outside a church: 'Rough seas make for good sailors. Smooth seas don't.' " When Eric is going biking, he'll say to Lisa, "I'm going on an adventure. Want to come along?" And Lisa enjoys her new physical fitness which permits her to join in the biking and hiking. They both agree the bad times have allowed them to appreciate the long run of good times. And they know that the power of their promise to each other gives them the ability to solve their problems, and to keep growing together.

Intimacy and Intensity

Kristina and Daniel needed to practice marriage, not in the sense of getting better at it, but in the Buddhist sense: incorporating its patterns and values with a long-term commitment to the process. Daniel's parents had divorced when he was 13. It was a traumatic event which made him swear that he would never marry or have children. When he and Kristina met, they were in their 30s. Kristina loved Daniel and wanted to have children. She felt the practical, biological reality that she was getting older. She and Daniel weren't ready for marriage, so they decided to have a child without marriage. After being parents for a year, they were ready to marry.

Daniel still felt that a wedding ceremony was a series of Thou Shalt Not commandments that enclosed one in the marital institution. He wanted a ceremony that would reflect his acceptance of Kristina and their daughter Kaya as an opening of energy into an evolving life together. Daniel had lived in Japan and practiced sitting meditation. When one learns meditation, one acknowledges the distractions of negative thoughts, but puts one's energy on the positive. To Kristina, this practice felt like a process which said, "You are encouraged to do so," as opposed to "You will refrain from doing." There was a well-known Zen center near her home in Santa Fe, and she suggested that they ask the priests there to officiate at their ceremony.

To anyone who imagines the traditional American white wedding, the ceremony at the Zen center will seem like a hippy cartoon: The baldheaded nun striking her clackers, the beating drum, and the toddler waddling about the edges of the ceremony. These images are unfamiliar and discordant, because we are used to the sacred as being separate from our daily lives. Daniel and Kristina saw their ceremony as a moment in a progressive line of moments that were and would be their lives — an evolving and ephemeral moment. Their promise to each other was to face life full on and avoid judgments. Kristina describes it as "an attempt not to make the bad things happen and to try to make the good things happen."

Even the nun's ritual clacker was a symbolic reminder to be present in the moment without judgment.

"Music affects us. Sound affects us," Kristina explains. "When you heard that clack, it was like a lightning strike. It was a commitment to pursuing the ambiguous. It was saying, 'You will resolve things. You have to follow what's real. If you stray, come back. So you get angry at each other. Come back and speak to each other.' You have to let yourself flow through the transgressions, the things that aren't ideal, that enter your life. Instead of grabbing hold of them, you let go, and you can come back to your committed, to your love, and honor that."

This simple ceremony was essentially a series of questions about the hopes and intentions that had brought Daniel and Kristina to this point. The nun struck her clackers together with each response. She wasn't stamping and finalizing their answers, she was energizing and giving mindfulness to the present. By doing so, the ceremony served to clarify their understanding of who they were to each other, and how they must act towards each other in the future.

The ceremony, however, was not marriage counseling; the clack was a symbol of awareness. The ritual served to emphasize the obligations which were already known to both Daniel and Kristina.

"Our relationship would have been different if we hadn't gone through the ritual," says Kristina. "I remember eight years ago, talking to someone and saying I am celebrating monogamy — and growing up in the '70s — that was a lot of hooey; but I think monogamy is important. It enriches my life with intimacy and intensity. It all goes back to remembering the clack." Kristina and Daniel feel that their ceremony has served as a foundation to a marriage that acknowledges what is happening, and by acknowledging the moment, gives entry to talking about the future.

Why do we marry?

A wedding ceremony is an expression of our human identity, at once an acknowledgement of both our physical and spiritual condition. As different as all my couples are, they all choose to have a wedding ceremony because they understand themselves within a pattern of family and community. Their deepest feelings for each other need to be expressed, not in isolation, but as a part of the universal continuum of birth, life, death and rebirth, the life cycle of the individual, the pattern of the four seasons, and the story of the great religions and myths. Why do we choose to marry? We are not complete when we are alone. Why do we have wedding ceremonies? Ritual is the tool our psyches create to understand our finite place in an infinite pattern. How do our wedding vows affect us? Words, having been said, do not disappear.

Our lives in 21st Century America are filled with practical considerations of time, and money, and convenience. These are the short-term considerations of our daily lives. But a wedding ceremony resonates long term, in concentric waves circling out into our lives, encircling time. The moment becomes all time, and time seems to fall out of step with its usual steady pace. That is why we say time stands still when we look into our loved one's eyes.

The distinction between quotidian time and ritual time needs to be reasserted when planning a wedding (or any life ceremony). Our words and ceremonies set us on a course into our future. Our choice of words affects the way we are seen, and how we see ourselves. These couples that I have described are more alike than different, for they all knew that the past enriches the future. In their ceremonies, they all draw upon cultural, spiritual, and personal images to construct unique expressions of their relationship to each other, and to their families and friends. For all of them, their marriages have echoed their wedding vows. A wedding ceremony is the story of what your life is becoming.

Why do we choose to marry? Why do we have a wedding ceremony? A poem from the Bhagavad Gita expresses the moment when we say our vows to each other:

Look to this day,
For it is life,
The very life of life.
In its brief course lie all the varieties
And realities of your existence;
The bliss of growth,
The glory of action,
The splendor of beauty,
For yesterday is but a dream,
And tomorrow is only a vision,
But today well lived makes
Every yesterday a dream of happiness
And every tomorrow a vision of hope.

Chapter Two

UNDERSTANDING RITUAL AND THE SPIRITUAL

Why has our secular society permitted conservative religion to hijack the word marriage? Ceremony doesn't belong to one belief system, and the nature of the human psyche demands a connection to a greater whole, whether through politics, religion, or superstition. A healthy culture needs to offer ritual to embody its citizens' abstract emotions and to provide structure for the intangible ties which give identity and connection.

My sister has two big dogs that stay on her property by means of an invisible electric fence. If they go too close to the boundary marker, their collars give them a mild shock. This conditioning results in self-policing. Approaching their boundary marker creates so much anxiety that, in fact, the dogs never try to wander. The power need not even be on.

So it is with our legislatures across the country. They have all been trained to assume that, if they tread too closely to the boundaries of accepted religion, they will be jolted back by a political shock. Thus, they ignore the true social and economic needs of the 21st Century because of the power of religious pressure groups. I am not anti-religious, just anti-dogmatic. Our marriage laws (determined state by state) remain locked into structures and terms that no longer have meaning to many couples. I believe the time has come for a new interpretation of marriage separated from any particular religious path or procedure.

In doing so, we must recognize the multi-layered needs of a long-term domestic relationship. Marriage is a close and intimate union entered into with the intention to last for the rest of the partners' lives. It should be a reflection of our American social order with all its diversity, mobility, and humanity. It involves legal rights and responsibilities, as well as emotional commitment far beyond the romantic image of falling in love. It is not static, but has changed significantly over the centuries. It is unique to each couple. For any group to claim that their way of wedding is the right way is hypocritical and narrow, either ignorant or intentionally blind to the many ways different cultures and couples choose life partners.

In fact, marriage, like most legal registries in the U.S., involves the accumulation of property. We live in a capitalist society. Property and choice are keystones of the political and social structure. Ownership and future rights to property are a primary reason to control the right to marry. No one would argue that a citizen could not go to a certain school, or buy a certain house, or shop in a certain store, or choose a certain profession. How, then, can we argue that we want to restrict the choosing of life partners and the accompanying responsibilities of health and property decisions that go with that choice?

In a perfectly rational society, marriage would be nothing but a contract determining the economic particulars of the merger. (In fact, the very rich who have access to lawyers ensure these rights of property with prenuptial agreements/contracts that refine the repercussions of marriage as determined by current legislation.) So why not have everyone go to the city clerk, sign a book, and be done with it? Because marriage and weddings have much more resonance in our lives than the fact of a license, even if licensing with careful records is necessary for sharing and transferring wealth. For most of us, there is a greater need to be served than protection of property.

Words have power — as much as a bolt of electricity. The arguments over marriage (much as there used to be arguments over the rights of divorce) are not based in reason. They are based in the emotional investment we have in the ceremony. No matter how ardently a rational secularist might argue of no need for ceremony, the truth is that the human psyche demands it and will construct it no matter how sparse the trappings. Let us then legally reconstitute our marriage laws and wedding customs. Let's recognize secular spirituality as well as religious spirituality, giving couples of all kinds the ability to have a life passage filled with the importance of their choice and the intention of their commitment. Let the churches, synagogues, mosques and temples choose the rites and words as their faith sees fit, but (for God's sake) let us give the secular an equal chance to celebrate the human spirit.

Having made the plea, let me qualify the term *secular spirituality.* It is not my invention. Dally Messenger, the Australian Civil Celebrant, has used it extensively, and a search on the Internet shows that others have done so, too. I approach the term as an artist. I became a marriage officiant because I am a storyteller, performing in modern times what has been done throughout the ages — entertaining and teaching by standing and sharing narratives, real and imagined. When I tell stories, my audiences inevitably give me new stories in response. I read folklore and myth from around the world. I listen to personal stories. I create stories from my own life. This artistic profession has given me a profound respect for the powerful effect of a story on the individual and collective psyche.

Art transforms a personal vision into a universal statement. Art cannot exist in isolation, but needs the collaboration of the viewer as well as the artist. We open ourselves up to the experience which the artist offers, and we are transformed by new ways of perceiving ourselves and our world. The artist's craft is to know the techniques developed over millennia, and to reinvent conventional structures, enabling the psyche to expand and understand the new facts being presented.

This explanation may seem terribly intellectual, but, in fact, for me, the process is totally emotional. It's built into the basic story which we experience every day, and which is the basis of most religions — birth, life, death and rebirth — the seasonal change of time; but we do not need to conceptualize a divinity to understand that this world is finite, and only time and change are infinite. All we need do is use our five senses. Thus, the artist/storyteller takes those sensory experiences and formulates them, so they can be incorporated into the personal and cultural story of our own lives. The listener then understands the human experience as fragile and awesome, small and great. The great 18th Century philosopher Edmund Burke calls this experience *the sublime*. This is what I term a spiritual experience.

The officiant's art is to create a ceremonial structure which celebrates our life passages and concentrates the sublime into a moment of life transition. As an artist, the civil celebrant listens to the particulars of the wedding couple's lives, then connects them through words, music, and movement into a story relating the universal passage of our lives from birth, to death, to a new generation taking its place. The officiant uses words to create a magic circle — similar to the power assigned to the religious altar or the magical alchemical circle — in which conventional time is suspended (Have you ever sat through an entertainment and thought it took no time?). We are transformed into a new stage of life: in a wedding two become one.

The power of this art does not have to be assigned to a set liturgy or divine structure. It works because it tells the story of all of us through the particulars of one of us — Thus, it is spiritual, if not religious, providing a paradox: It touches the most basic experiences we can have, acknowledging the world's ephemeral nature; and yet it recognizes the infinity of variations, and the seemingly endless generations that have gone before us and will follow us.

If we set our life's course by reason, without heart, we steer toward nihilism. Nothing lasts. But we cannot ignore our connection to others. So our heart creates ritual to reinforce that even though we are only a small part of humanity, each of us has a unique part to play in the continuum. The ceremony gives us hope, and we see that the world is renewed.

I cannot say that I believe in miracles, but I do believe that the spirit has power beyond the rational, and that energy is released through our connections to each other. I was trained as an actor and writer to understand that behavior makes the imaginary real. As a wedding celebrant, I have discovered that behavior, in the form of ritual, fills reality with the power of creative imagination. When we marry, we release the potential to imagine the future we want, and if we can imagine it, we can reach for it. Certain stories come to me as touchstones. My friend Yaffa Eliach provides one such in her book *Hasidic Tales of the Holocaust* which I adapted into a musical play, "Dancing With Miracles."

In the Nazi concentration camps, a rabbi and an atheist became close friends, bonding by feeding each other on stories of wonderful meals that they enjoyed before the war. Often, they would argue over whether or not there was a God and, if so, what kind of God could create this hell they were experiencing. One night, as the prisoners were sleeping on their hard wooden bunks, the lights suddenly came on. "Out with you," shouted the guards. "Quickly, run into the fields." The prisoners in a panic that they might be shot on the spot ran into the cold night, only to discover the ruse. In the middle of the field, a machine gun tower and spotlight had been mounted at the side of a bomb crater. The prisoners were told to remove their clothing and jump across the pit. If they fell into the pit, they would be shot and it would be their grave. The pit was as wide as a two lane street. No one could reach the other side. The atheist said to the rabbi, "Why be the butt of their joke? Let us sit here and be shot." The rabbi said to the atheist, "No, my friend, if it is decreed that we must jump, then jump we must." And so they moved forward to the edge of the pit. Suddenly, they were borne aloft and landed on the other side.

"How can it be?" the atheist cried. "What magic is this that we are alive? Rabbi, for your sake, I am alive. How did you do it?"

"My friend," said the rabbi, "I held on to the coattails of my father, and grandfather, and all my ancestors. But you? How did you do it?"

"Rabbi," replied the atheist, "I held on to you."

Yaffa, who is a historian, found a photograph of the bomb crater. It *was* as wide as a two lane street.

Time and again, life takes us to a place of impossibility, and we must choose to leap, believing in the strength of our connection to family and friends. I am giving you the big stories, but everyone's story is a miracle. We stand on the edge, and the choice we make to leap or not to leap determines our fate. If it seems eccentric to tell a story of war and hatred in a wedding book, I do so because our commercial culture tiptoes around the hardest choices of life and death, and deceives us with conventional choices. Marriage is for better or worse until death do us part, and those traditional vows hold the truth of the feeling. The magic of a wedding ceremony is not that things do not end, but that by recognizing death, we choose life, to leap over the pit.

Usually, we do not even recognize the intrinsic magic taking place in the choices we make and the formulae we live out. I always look forward to asking my clients about their wedding proposals. Ninety-nine per cent of the couples tell me they had already talked about getting married, knew they would be married, and simply acceded to the cultural expectation that it was up to the man to ask the question. Ninety-nine per cent of the men also tell me that they tried to make it a surprise and a perfect beginning to a perfect future. Few really appreciate the poetic imagery of their story. They tell me they have no story until it is revealed through ceremony.

Recently, I had a young couple with three children ask me to plan their ceremony. They had no practical reason to get married. They were financially able to live together and raise their children in the tabloid style of a Hollywood star; but they weren't satisfied to have only legal and financial security. They wanted their children to hear the words that expressed what they felt for each other, and what they hoped for their family. They were at once bursting with romance. (After all, they were finally getting married.) At the same time, they were desperately trying to stay low-key. They insisted that they had no story to tell. Just two people who loved each other and wanted to raise children. Only when I asked about their proposal night, did they reveal themselves. "Oh, we went to the top of the Empire State Building," they told me. I laughed, "Like Sleepless in Seattle?" "No," the groom replied. "I never saw that movie. Is the Empire State Building in it? I took her there because it was high up and open late." One of the great sights of the world is the night view from the Empire State Building, across the lights of New York City, into the limitless horizon. "You wanted a place of infinite possibilities?" I asked. He smiled, "Probably something like that."

We rarely realize (and sometimes don't want to admit) the power that symbols and words have over us, even as they make us greater than ourselves. On one of the most important nights of their lives, the groom wanted to go with his bride to the top of the world. Only when I told the story, did he understand his feelings and dreams.

One of my favorite weddings involved a middle-aged couple both of whom had unhappy first marriages. One story ended with a suicide; the other story was a tale of mean-spirited betrayal and divorce. They had each mourned for two years, and then decided to join a ballroom dance class in order to get back in circulation. One night, they met as part of a snowball dance in which partners keep choosing new partners; but this time they broke the rules and stayed with each other. Months later, when the groom chose a time and place for the marriage proposal, it was on Valentine's Day, and the dance company created a special evening to frame the event. For the culmination of the wedding ceremony (which of course was at the dance hall), after the "I now pronounce you husband and wife" and the "You may kiss," the couple began to dance a waltz, beginning a snowball dance that ended with all the guests twirling around the floor in celebration. This couple, who had been through so much, was affirming in their marriage the possibility of renewal. They invited us all to join with them in the dance of life: dipping, twirling, and stepping to a classical pattern filled with feeling. I, the storyteller, saw Cinderella and the Prince dancing at a ball that could continue for the rest of their lives.

A lovely young couple came to me with their story of a Hawaiian proposal. They had both been downsized and decided that they would embrace unemployment by going off together to a tropical paradise for three months. About six weeks into this romantic retreat, the groom arranged a tour to a waterfall in the middle of the jungle. Here, he planned to propose. Afraid that he might lose the engagement ring in the water, he ordered a plastic diamond via the Internet. When they arrived, they walked from the helicopter through the wild and emerged into magic. The site was breathtakingly beautiful: Wild orchids growing on swaying trees; water lapping against rocks; the sparkling stream falling from high above. They climbed up on the ledge and the bride said, "I can't jump. The water will be too cold." The groom replied, "We haven't come this far to turn back. Plunge." And together they leaped into a Paradise both inviting and frightening. When they emerged the groom was holding the ersatz ring. "What's that?" asked the bride. "Something you got on the Internet?" the bride said with some contempt. "Will you marry me, even if I don't have diamonds to give you?" replied the groom. She thought for a second and said yes. That evening, they took a windjammer cruise. As the world turned golden, he gave her a real diamond, and they sailed off into the sunset.

The old stories have survived because they tell the truth about life. We plunge into the waters that test us, and emerge able to see our true love. Life forces us to sit in the ashes, and then our prince comes. We will climb to the highest heights for our true love. Everyone has a story, even if we do not find ourselves in a beautiful setting with leisure and money. Everyone has the advantage of the poetic imagination to inspire and embody the power of their lives. The sun rises and sets everywhere. Couple after couple come to me with a story to tell, filled with storybook images. Celebrants of any kind, religious or civil, should be giving voice to these dream-like visions, turning them through ceremony into the substance of your new life. Your officiant and your ceremony should tell your story.

In the 1980s, I worked with Robert Alexander, the artistic director of the Living Stage in Washington, D.C. Bob used to say, "We are all geniuses. Our job as artists is to bring out the genius in all of us." In our status-conscious and competitive society, we think of genius as extraordinary intelligence a la Einstein, an ability reserved to the few to do what most of us are incapable of doing. Einstein's genius, however, wasn't so much the depth of his knowledge as the leaps he was willing to take from the edge of the known into the unknown. His great theory of relativity started in a dream: he saw himself riding on a beam of light. From that dream, he re-imagined the universe. We can all dream.

On the day that we marry, we live a dream. We pretend to be kings and queens, and for that moment everyone treats us as the royal couple with all the trappings. Why shouldn't we also pretend to be geniuses and give ourselves the opportunity to reimagine the world together? Imagine if we started to live our stories? Imagine the strength we could draw from each other to face the tests that inevitably come before us. We can all be geniuses, even if we feel incapable of being Einstein. We need only believe in our imaginations and the power of words.

The ancient Indian parable tells of a water bearer who carries two pots on his shoulder. One pot is perfect. The other pot is cracked. Day after day, year after year, the water bearer draws water from the well and carries the filled pots to his stall in the market. Day after day, year after year, the perfect pot arrives full, but the flawed pot arrives half empty. Finally, ashamed for his imperfection, the flawed pot apologizes that he has wasted so much of the water bearer's effort. "My friend," the water bearer replies, "you must not feel less for who you are. Look at the path we have walked together. Where I carry the perfect pot by my side, the road is dry and hard. But on your side, flowers bloom to lift my heart and quicken my steps." Imagine the power of a ceremony that reveals the potential of words that we often let dribble away.

Such a ceremony was Keri and Bill's. As a teenager, Keri had often seen Bill, an "older man" in his twenties ride by on his bicycle. She thought he was cute and her family teased her about him. Years passed, Bill had become a recent widower with three children, and Keri was their swimming coach. Knowing the story of the family tragedy, Keri befriended the children who quickly became a connection between Keri and Bill. Caring for others soon became caring for each other, and what had seemed a huge age difference at 17 was not so great at 27. Still, the prospect of marrying an instant family and of inheriting the legacy of a dead mother who had been adored by both husband and children was daunting.

Keri did not deny the fear of inheriting this family. Instead, she faced it head on. So, we acknowledged the tragic beginnings of this relationship, along with the disparity in their ages. Surmounting these challenges tested and strengthened their feelings for one another, even while they shared a common goal to care for the children. Their love, born of a shared responsibility toward the children, now united all five members of the family in a powerful bond. The ceremony touched on the past, making the present celebration seem even sweeter, and heralding an even brighter future.

Ceremony

Morgan, Dempsey, and Devon, please come up here and hold hands, forming a circle of love with your father and Keri.

Today is the beginning of a great new chapter in all your lives.

Love isn't a decision. It's a feeling. If we could decide who we loved, it would be much simpler, but much less magical. We are given our families, and in sharing, discover the specialness of each other. This evening, we formalize that Keri and Bill will be husband and wife and that all five of you will be a family. Family isn't about whose blood you have. It's about who you care about. Keri and Bill affirm today that you three will always be a special part of their shared life. Life may bring bitter as well as sweet, but wherever you go, whatever you do, this moment of looking at each other as we all look into your future together, will be a reminder that you are one family.

Keri will read:

We are a family now, a whole,
Of which you are a part,
And you are just as much my children
As any in my heart.

I do not love you differently,
Nor would I give up less
Of all that life has given me
To bring you happiness.

There is no limit to my love,
No boundary you might cross,
No price you might be asked to pay,
No need to fear its loss.

We are now one, the five of us,
Windows of one home.
As long as I have life and breath,
You'll never be alone.

Keri and Bill, as a lasting reminder of the vows you will make to each other tonight and the circle of love which makes you one, you have printed a statement of your promises to each other which I now ask you to sign and your family to witness. It says:

In the presence of the Love of their families and friends we promise to be a loving and supportive family to one another for tomorrow, today, and forever. We promise to cherish and delight in our spirit and individuality, to respect our differences, and to face life's challenges with patience, humor, and kindness. This commitment is made in love, kept in faith, lived in hope, and made eternally new.

In celebration of this commitment we set our hands.

Keri and Bill sign

Each of the children sign as Gerry calls them
Morgan, Dempsey, and Devon

Children stand behind unity candle

Keri and Bill, I ask you now to light the Unity Candle.

This flame represents the spirit that burns in each of us and in all living things. This flame represents the eternal whose strength is the connection that endures in memory and love and is passed on through marriage and children and family and community.

They light candles as Gerry continues.

There is a quotation from Helen Keller, "The best and most beautiful things in the world cannot be seen or even touched. They must be felt with the heart." The flame you light as one represents the intangible energy of love that cannot be measured, but burns within your soul. This flame represents the caring and giving that you pledge to each other today; this spark of light which you pass to each other becomes ever stronger from this day forth, as it burns as one.

The words which you say to each other this evening are only breath, but they are the most beautiful things in the world, for they are felt truly with all your heart.

Bill's sister Tara will read a passage by Edmund O'Neill:

TARA:
Marriage is a commitment to life, the best that two people can find and bring out in each other. It offers opportunities for sharing and growth that no other relationship can equal. It is a physical and an emotional joining that is promised for a lifetime.

Within the circle of its love, marriage encompasses all of life's most important relationships. A wife and a husband are each other's best friend, confidant, lover, teacher, listener, and critic. And there may come times when one partner is heartbroken or ailing, and the love of the other may resemble the tender caring of a parent for a child.

Marriage deepens and enriches every facet of life. Happiness is fuller, memories are fresher, commitment is stronger, even anger is felt strongly, and passes away more quickly.

Marriage understands and forgives the mistakes life is unable to avoid. It encourages and nurtures new life, new experiences, and new ways of expressing a love that is deeper than life.

When two people pledge their love and care for each other in marriage, they create a spirit unique unto themselves which binds them closer than any spoken or written words. Marriage is a promise, a potential made in the hearts of two people who love each other and takes a lifetime to fulfill.

GERRY:

Keri says of Bill that he has taught her what true love is. Bill says of Keri that all he wants in his life is to make sure that her dreams come true.

Morgan, Dempsey and Devon, this story could not have happened without you. Keri met your father because she was your swimming coach. She cared for you when you needed a friend, and soon through you she became your father's friend as well. But friendship grew into love as Keri and Bill saw the kindness and concern they each held at the core of their beings. Two souls who were meant for each other.

For his wedding proposal, Bill wanted the perfect ring. He chose one and then felt it wasn't good enough. He finally had a specially designed ring made to present to Keri. While on vacation in Jamaica, he had a candlelight dinner prepared for her on the beach. At the dinner he presented her with a pair of earrings. He then said, "I have something else that will go with them." He then knelt before Keri and asked, "Will you marry me?" And truly, the words were more precious than any jewel.

The happy ending of your story is tonight as you become husband and wife and a family. You called it a leap of faith, but I think it is the richness of your dreams coming true.

In the center of the Cathedral in Siena, Italy, there is a mosaic portrait of Hermes Trismegistus. In medieval Europe, the cult of Hermes influenced such diverse thinkers as St. Augustine, Cosimo de' Medici, the Knights Templar, and eventually the Freemasons. Hermes supposedly was an Egyptian priest who through words and ritual could incorporate the energy of the universe to make inanimate objects move. He is the father of Alchemy, the magic that can turn lead into gold. The hermetic tradition believes that self-awareness and purification are necessary for magic to happen. At this point, don't get stuck in literal thinking, but imagine the power of ceremony focusing our awareness, refining the moment and turning the lead of life into gold, as Keri and Bill did.

I believe that when the real stories are told, life and love purify us, and the ensuing self-awareness frees our genius to recognize our lives as truly precious moments. Ceremony gives us the opportunity to step away from the leaden realities of everyday life into the imaginative gold of what can be — like Einstein's light beam — the key to understanding time and using it well. I believe that ritual focuses us into the alchemical circle. Just as an actor makes the imaginary real by doing, so the officiant makes the hopes and dreams of the assembly real by organizing a ceremony into ritual structure. There is no literal power in a glass of wine, a taste of sweet rice, a beating drum or ringing bell, a candle lit or incense burnt; but all these symbols and sensory images of ritual focus our attention. They take our concentration off ourselves and place it onto the universal story being told; and that story opens our feelings to laughter, and tears, and love, and to the truth of our hearts.

From my observation, ritual seems to follow a very similar pattern throughout humanity. There is the calling in of the assembly and the acknowledgement of the ritual space, the statement of faith, the incorporation of spiritual power, the celebration of the special moment with a blessing, the promise, and the sending forth. Appropriate readings and stories are interspersed to accent and energize the stages of celebration. This pattern focuses power into the magic circle. The assembled begin to breathe as one, and the officiant becomes the voice of the universal.

I'm not a theologian. I'm a storyteller and an actor, but I have seen this pattern used in theater, dance, ceremony and oratory to create a heightened spiritual state, a suspension of our everyday world, and a vision in which the imaginary becomes real. As artists, we choose the words to include the rhythms as well as the images most potent to our community. Language is musical. The ancient bards sang their stories. The ritual formula is supported by the orality of words and composition. The ceremony is written to be heard, and, just as our language has changed from generation to generation, so must the spoken rhythms of the ceremony.

Have you ever noticed the self-conscious cadence of ministers or rabbis who singsong their way through a service? I don't think it works very well; but the similarity of style makes me suspect that, at some time in every seminary, a speech course has taught these patterns as effective public speaking. I have wondered why and have come to conclude that in academic situations, the need for emotional craft is underestimated. The acolyte is taught information and a systematic approach to preaching that can be massfitted to all graduates. The preacher learns patterns that are good enough indications if the story is already somewhere in the assembled shared experience.

Indeed, stentorian cadences do make one assign authority. Uniformity in words, rhythms, and movement, do trigger automatic response. Say the right word and we automatically kneel, and our body memory brings forth the feelings we were taught in religious education. Just as commercial entertainment depends on formula and indication, so does the commercial art of liturgy. This reasoning is the causality of liturgy.

Decades and sometimes centuries ago, the academic and bureaucratic authorities of religion made choices to ensure that anyone could deliver a ceremony, and that no one would change the rules. Set liturgy depends on an accepted, even mandatory, formula to bring out the genius or spirit in us as a community; but when the conventional words lose their power, we must find new images that will connect us. Form and song must be supported by contemporary and personal meaning and truth.

I prefer fairly traditional words for the wedding vows. I find that the formula is so ingrained that guests will mouth the words as I say them.

I, — — — —, take you, — — — — —,
to be my wife
to have and to hold,
from this day forward,
for better or worse,
for richer or poorer,
in sickness and in health,
as long as we both shall live.

I use a straightforward and very simple setting of these sentiments, and, with this choice, I find everyone is encouraged to follow along. This is the most important moment of the ceremony, and I want everyone to be listening with their whole being. However, my job as a civil celebrant is to find the words and rhythms that belong to the couple. An English couple brought me two poems from the Purple Ronnie collection which they wanted to read as wedding vows.

BRIDE:

A Poem About How to be a Husband
Sometimes you've got to be macho
And do lots of things that are tough
But sometimes it's best to be quiet and gentle
And say lots of soppy type stuff

It's good to have hundreds of muscles
And girls always like a nice bum
But you mustn't be hairy or sweaty or fat
Or have any flab on your tum.

Don't ever talk about football
or make nasty smells in the bed
or joke about bosoms with mates in the pub
or drink till you're out of your head

You've got to be funny and clever
and do loads of things by surprise
like shouting out loud in the back of the bus
'my wife has got beautiful eyes'

Say to your wife "you're gorgeous
Your body's a twelve out of ten
You're sexy, and beautiful, clever, and kind"
Then tell her all over again.

GROOM:

A Poem About Love
You tell me I'm fat and I'm ugly
You tell me I'm utterly nuts
You tell me I burp and I fart and I smell
But that's why I love you so much.

Sometimes it makes you feel happy
And sometimes it makes you feel blue
But I find it makes me feel smashingly fab
And that's cos I'm in it with you.

Not my choice! But meaningful to the bride and groom and, because it was true to them, it brought laughter and charm to their wedding. Their guests, who were quite familiar with the doggerel poetry, were not put off, but felt included in a very personal moment, a moment of quiet whimsy. The surprise of a good ceremony is the magic revealed in the tiny truths as well as the great ones.

Not every moment need be pomp and pageantry. In fact, in our commercial age, pomposity has become fashionable, as the wedding industry tries to sell its own self-importance. Modern catering halls and bridal stylists try to pretend to create palaces and cathedrals, but the heart of wedding will always be two people saying a simple but fundamental vow of love to each other. Modern ritual depends not on the invincibility of dogma, but upon the vulnerability of truth. The ritual formula and the symbolic actions and words of ceremony are only tools to frame the essential humanity of the moment. The formulae of ritual are real, because they are the way humanity thinks and feels. The power of ceremony comes not from puffs of smoke, but from a simple and clear expression of a couple's love.

You must choose what is true to yourselves. A good officiant can guide you in this process and deliver the ceremony without getting in the way of the truth of who you are. Would it be easier to just take the words from a bridal magazine? Does it take effort on your part to participate in finding the right words to say "I do?" Of course, and I have couples contact me all the time asking for something short and simple. By this they mean that the words are not important. They just need someone to do the legal form and want to pay as little as possible to have me be their clerk. I reply I don't measure words by the yard; they are not sold by volume; but your words do reflect the weight of saying "I do," and as such, even a short, simple ceremony is precious.

Whatever your style, a wedding ritual should have more intention than a piece of legal paper awarded at the finish. The ceremony is not a dash to the party, it is the beginning of a journey through a new life. Give them careful consideration, because your words can launch you and sustain you. Your choice to be married is a public acknowledgement of your relationship. Don't be afraid to say, "Here we are and off we go." As Walt Whitman put it:

> *We will sail pathless and wild seas,*
> *We will go where winds blow, waves dash, and the Yankee*
> *Clipper speeds by under full sail.*
> *Allons! With power, liberty, the earth, the elements,*
> *Health, defiance, gayety, self-esteem, curiosity;*
> *Allons! From all formules!*
>
> *Camerado, I give you my hand!*
> *I give you my love more precious than money,*
> *I give you myself before preaching or law;*
> *Will you give me yourself? Will you come travel with me?*
> *Shall we stick by each other as long as we live?*

That is the heart of wedding.

Chapter Three

A HISTORY OF WEDDING: COMING DOWN THE AISLE ALL DRESSED IN WHITE

I was traveling in Rajastan, India, during wedding season. Every evening we would wait expectantly for the parades to begin. As dusk fell, we would begin to hear music and, with shouts of "It's coming from that direction," we would run down the street to catch the procession. Around the corner would come a painted elephant draped in glittering silver and gold, followed by a brass band and attendants holding colorful torches. The wedding guests followed behind the band, dancing to the music and pulling passers-by into the celebration. Finally, the groom, dressed like a maharajah, came riding atop a white stallion harnessed with elaborate ribbons and decorations. The procession would proceed to the bride's house and then escort her to the wedding ceremony, which always culminated in fireworks. Some nights the streets of a town held four or five such weddings at a time, and the horizon would have fireworks in every direction. We never tired of chasing weddings. The music, the lights, the costumes, made a joyous event that was the best theater in the world: the feelings were real and the event celebrated one of the happiest shared rituals in anyone's life. I was always disappointed that I couldn't see the rest of the story, for I know that a parade is only the tip of the Hindu rites.

This Momentous Moment

Everywhere in the world, people get married. For better or worse, for richer or poorer, all humanity seeks the connection between two people, and when that moment comes, everyone wants to celebrate with parades, and dancing, and fireworks. We follow a ritual because we are told it is the customary observance or practice. Often, when planning a wedding, contemporary American couples treat their party as the ritual, accepting the wedding industry's "right way to do it" as the explanation of the event. Buying this advice is a bit like thinking that the elephants and the horse are the core components of the Indian wedding. Instead, we should understand how and why the wedding industry has created the conventional wedding party and make informed decisions as we would with any major purchase. In the end, we can use the formulae of fashion to make the transformative moment when magic words are spoken the real center of the wedding ritual.

The momentous moment which affirms the completion of our search is not validated because of the party. Rather, the party affirms our community's rejoicing in its continuity. When your guests go home, they should not be talking about the food. They should be remembering the ceremony, and how it filled them with the importance of the event for the bride and groom and for themselves.

On February 11, 1840, England's Queen Victoria married Albert of Saxe-Coburg at the royal chapel of St James in London. Although royal brides would customarily wear red and brocade, the Queen, following the fashion of the day, dressed in white satin trimmed with orange blossoms. Although white had been used since ancient times for ritual events, it was by no means the common costume of a bride; but for the Victorians it was a charming indication of fragile femininity. On her head, but not covering her face, was a veil of lace, a headpiece also interpreting the style of the moment. (The satin and Honiton lace she wore were produced by English mills that had helped make her empire the richest in the world. Like any good, modern populist politician, Victoria was conscious of promoting her constituency's product and shoring up her popularity by demonstrating that she was just a regular guy.) Since she lived in Buckingham Palace, the Queen needed to travel by coach to the chapel where Albert was waiting. She was escorted by 12 bridesmaids. This spectacle was an ideal picture to engrave and sell to the public and was distributed worldwide. Thus, with the attendant publicity of Victoria and Albert's celebrity wedding, a white gown and veil became a fashionable choice that, over the next century and a half, would be made into the symbol of brides throughout the world. The modern wedding and all its expensive details merely mimics this event 170 years ago, with a little help from modern media, advertising and even Walt Disney.

Romantics and Capitalists

The Victorians were both romantics and capitalists. Therefore, the wedding that descends from them represents a tension between the impulse for self expression and the philosophy of commoditization. The industrial revolution created middle-class wealth and, with wealth, education. The poets and novelists of the 19th Century popularized the concept of personal happiness. Novelists such as Austen, Dickens, Thackery, and Trollop presented middle-class heroes and heroines who could love as deeply as any prince or princess. Until the 19th Century and, in fact, into the 20th Century, the concepts of love and certainly lust were separate from marriage. Few couples would have considered a love match as a necessary component for marriage. In fact, the basis of romantic love, the traditions of courtly love, the idealization of the lady by the knight, was not intended as a basis for marriage. It was an indulgence of the upper class and the leisure class. The idealized lady was unavailable, and, often, married to someone else.

Marriage, as opposed to love, was a civil contract intended to stabilize society. It provided a structure for the transfer of property for those who possessed wealth, and the division of labor for those who worked; and even to this day, the basic legal aspect of a wedding ceremony is to have two witnesses hear the bride and groom agree to be married; this ensures the validity of the contract by which we regulate estate transfers, employment benefits, name registries, visitation rights, and life and death decisions in hospitals. Clergy did not become a necessary part of the marriage ceremony until the Council of Trent in 1563 at the end of the Middle Ages when the church shored up its political power by requiring a church-supervised wedding ceremony. Thus, the venue of the ceremony became associated with religion, and the central authority at the ceremony became the priest.

In the 19th Century, however, technology began to create mass publications with pictures which could spread a new idea and dictate fashion. At the same time, the rise of the department store provided distribution of mass-produced goods suddenly made available by new inventions housed in large factories. Over the course of the century from Victoria's wedding to World War II, the stage was set to expand the wedding ritual so that it would emphasize the consumer rewards of *getting* married as opposed to the spiritual rewards of *being* married.

A Coronation

America was the center of this new attitude with its nouveau-riche society striving to become nobility. In 19th Century America, one could buy authority, literally transporting old Europe lock, stock, and barrel back home. Industrialists who built great fortunes on lumber, silver, gold, railroads — the labor of the common man — bought the castles of old world aristocracy and shipped them stone by stone to become the mansions of the New World. By the second half of the century, not only could one buy the halls and trappings of nobility, but when the daughters of the wealthy were ready to marry, they could make a match with a European count, or duke, or prince, and ship the titles and history back home to the family in America. Thus, the wedding was not only a union, but in some respects a coronation.

This concept was cemented into the public consciousness at the end of the century by a series of highly publicized power weddings. In 1893, Prince George of York (later George V of England and Emperor of India) married Mary of Teck (who would become Queen Mary). As almost a bookend to her own wedding half a century before, the now elderly Queen Victoria rode through the adoring crowds of London to attend her grandson's celebrations. Two years later in New York, Consuelo Vanderbilt, a princess of New York society, married the Duke of Marlborough, an old-world royal. The American press loved the story. The publicity was so intense that *The New York Times* filled its news columns with descriptions of the bride's trousseau down to the underwear, 14 sets of cambric corsets trimmed with Valenciennes lace and embroidered with "Consuelo" on the ribbons. By the turn of the century, the grand "royal" wedding had become de rigueur. In 1906, Alice Roosevelt, daughter of President Theodore Roosevelt, was married in the White House. Even in the People's House, the wedding festivities were extravagant. Rumor has it that some of the thousands of gifts received and displayed as part of the wedding festivities are still in storage in some Washington sub-basement.

Ritual, however, does not travel in a direct line. Many other layers of custom and experience determine the conventions that we now follow where the bride is queen for the day, a delicate flower who must be given away by her father to another man. Perhaps, one of the more entertaining historical precedents for modern wedding customs is P. T. Barnum's promotion of the wedding of General Tom Thumb to Miss Lavinia Warren in 1863. In the midst of the Civil War, the American public was captivated by the images of the diminutive couple (bride and groom were each less than three feet tall) marrying just like royalty.

Barnum's genius was to take a private moment and make it public. Unlike kings and queens, most people at that time would have thought it unseemly to be gawked at and photographed at a personal ceremony. Barnum planted the seed, later nurtured by the Hollywood studios, which grew into today's fascination with celebrity lives as a source for emulation and titillation. The photos of Tom Thumb and his bride were distributed across the nation. The story was told and retold. The idea that even the littlest of us could aspire to be married in high fashion became ingrained in the popular culture. The pleasure and excitement of regular folks sharing images of themselves, just like the higher-ups, became a forerunner of modern public relations and the beginning of the custom of the wedding album.

Diamonds are Forever

Thus, you can see that the style of the modern wedding is an accumulation of history and cultural choices. In order to make your wedding what you want it to be and have it say what you want it to say, let us deconstruct the pattern of the traditional wedding ceremony. Let's discuss how and why we can use these rituals to make them not only of the past, but also of today.

Our human intelligence sees symbolic meaning everywhere, but the symbol takes its meaning from context, not from totemic power. For instance, the diamond ring only became set as the symbol of an engagement in 1947 when Frances Geretty, a copywriter for A.W. Ayers and Sons, created the brilliant slogan "A Diamond Is Forever" for DeBeers Mining. Until that time, the diamond market had been mostly industrial. There was an oversupply of the stones, and De Beers, who held a monopoly on the product, wanted a new market. By connecting the romantic sense of undying love with a stone that cannot be destroyed, Geretty created the perfect symbol which almost everyone could afford at least once in their lives, and which would never be resold. In truth, diamonds have very poor resale value and, if everyone tried to sell their diamonds, the market would crash. We don't buy diamonds as an investment, but for the story we believe they tell. Token rings had often been exchanged at engagements before this time; but with the De Beers campaign, the diamond ring became the standard to demonstrate an enduring bond, and De Beers was assured of a never-ending and profitable outlet for its gems.

Similarly, go to Tiffany's and the salesperson will tell you that that the classic wedding invitation should be heavy white stock engraved in black with a very formal request by the parents of the bride. A second smaller card is included for the reception with a tissue separating the two cards. Of course, this style has nothing to do with today's manners, but harkens back to a time before modern printing techniques and to an era when society weddings would have many more guests at the ceremony than at the reception. The select few would receive a second card to invite them to the more intimate second gathering. The tissue was placed between the cards so the ink wouldn't smudge. Today, this style is a charming and a highly profitable anachronism.

Past, Present and Future

I am not urging the desertion of all these customs. They have obtained meaning by usage. I am urging, however, that while making plans for a wedding ceremony, we not feel constrained by the blinders imposed by the arbiters of the wedding industry. From procession to recession, a wedding ceremony should symbolize the people who are marrying and the families being joined. A ceremony should contain the energy that convenes community and should symbolize the flowing of past, present and future into one shared current. When convention serves, use it. When something new is needed, don't be afraid. There are no wedding police.

The Opening Passage

Consider the procession. Some grooms wish to simply appear from a side door. Possibly this idea comes from the physical fact that in many churches there are robing rooms on the side of the chancel. When weddings only involved the couple and witnesses, one might wait quietly in one of these rooms and chat with the pastor. Historically, groomsmen became more important as the wedding ceremony grew into a large number of people and ushers were needed to control the crowds. Thus, the custom rose for the groom to arrive with an escort of men. The image of the groom and his men arriving together to march down the aisle harkens back to ancient days when brides were prizes of war and bands of men would go off to capture women. I always find this moment a bit silly. Thus, in hotels and catering halls where there are rarely ways to enter except for the men to come down the aisle at the head of the procession, I recommend that they serve as escorts to the bridesmaids. To my taste, this later choice makes an elegant picture which symbolizes the community of peers who are witnessing the changing lives of their friends. In Jewish weddings, the groom is escorted by his parents. I have always liked that gesture, seeing it as the groom respectfully seating his parents and, then, demonstrating that he is independently awaiting his bride.

However, many brides want their bridesmaids to be a solitaire as they come down the aisle. Emotionally, this acknowledges their unique connection to the bride. In fact, the style results from the linking of weddings with beauty contests and fashion shows. The bridemaid's matching ensemble was a stylistic creation of the 1920s and 1930s when simple fashion and mass production permitted off-the-rack buying. Department stores like B. Altman's of New York created bridal salons in which everything could be bought from one merchant, and "necessities" were invented to encourage sales. The bridal salon mimicked the couture collections of Paris with models showing dresses to the prospective brides. Merchants soon realized that they could sell additional dresses to the entire bridal party and began to stock styles for the bride's attendants.

After World War II, wedding salons sprung up across America. At the same time, beauty contests, especially the Miss America contest, began to capture the public fancy. As anyone who grew up in 20th Century America knows, a high point of the contest was the parade of potential queens in their ball gowns. When the Queen is finally crowned, the runners-up become her attendants. Although Miss Americas are required to be unmarried, by 1961, Nancy Anne Fleming, one of the most popular winners of the contest, was posing in a bridal gown for Brides magazine. The subliminal connections of walking down the aisle and walking down the runway were fused.

There are no definitive formulas to follow when arranging the procession. Western tradition puts the bride's party on the left; but Jews reverse this custom, I assume because the Hebrew alphabet is read right to left. Sometimes parents and even grandparents precede the procession. As an officiant, I find it necessary to enter before the processional music begins in order to remind everyone to turn off their cell phones. Some couples think this announcement is tacky, but a chorus of ring tones always results as a prelude to the procession. The choices of how to organize your wedding party's entrance into the ceremony can be any permutation which fits your style. The formula only matters so long as it finally says what needs to be said; i.e. this is a moment of crossing over, of lives entering a new space. Whether descended from Queen Victoria entering the chapel or Nancy Fleming walking down the runway, the concept of creating a procession is set because it symbolizes much more than its historical precedents. Whatever stylistic choices are made, I always find it thrilling to see the procession coming down the aisle. It is the opening passage of a story that will go on for a lifetime.

A Symbol of Hope

I believe hope is why the color we have come to associate with weddings is white. Most people associate white with purity and, therefore, think the bride wears white as a symbol of virginity. Since a majority of couples have been living together for at least a year, I doubt that symbol applies any more. Instead, I think white symbolizes a clean slate, a fresh start, the purity of beginning a new stage of life unblemished by the past. There is nothing as hopeful as a wedding, and white is a symbol of hope. The groomsmen and bridesmaids come in, not to show themselves off, but to be witnesses to the hope that the bride and groom place in each other. Therefore, the ritual space is energized by the wedding party both as they enter, and by their inclusion in some aspect of the ceremony, whether a reading, a signing, or a presentation. One of the most meaningful ceremonies I have written included a moment when the bride and groom received a symbolic flower from each of their attendants and, in turn, stated the reason that each was included in this intimate life passage — because they laughed together, grew together, worked together, and dreamed together.

At the end of the procession, the bride enters escorted by her father or a male relative. Traditionally, the guests rise when the bride arrives. Obviously, one stands for the Queen. In fact, I think it is harder to see the bride when everyone is standing. However, there is a theatrical excitement generated by the announcement of "Please rise for the bride," with its swelling music. Some choices should go beyond utility. I do have to ask why it is only a male who gives the bride away? The tradition of the father giving the bride away is obviously grounded in the ancient concept of bride sales. The Jews have both parents walking in with their daughter, and I have found that many modern brides appreciate the power of this symbol. This moment is all about family dynamics. I have worked with modern brides who preferred to leave their male escort and walk forward on their own to meet the groom. Such gestures may seem petty or feminist, but the impulse is powerful and the symbol important.

We become by doing. When we create ritual, we are creating the images which inform our lives. Better to renew those images so they truly represent who we are than to mimic images that no longer have meaning and eventually will become emotionally hollow.

An Exchange of Breath

Once the bride and groom are standing together, they often light a Unity Candle. Probably the most-observed ritual in an American wedding, this semi-religious moment was first popularized in the 1980s by fundamentalist protestant churches. The widespread popularity of this ritual speaks to the powerful image it invokes. Many traditions use candles or open flames. Fire is life. Fire is transformation and rebirth. Jews bless candles. Hindus walk around the fire four times. Zoroastrians see fire as a symbol of purification and rebirth. When the bride and groom light one candle from two, the symbol tells the story and gives a lovely picture as well. Some officiants place the candle at the end of the ceremony after the vows. I feel it is better placed at the opening of the ceremony. The whole ceremony is a series of unifying moments leading up to the voicing of the vows. That exchange of breath is the most powerful moment of the wedding. Anything thereafter is an anticlimax.

Ethereal and Elemental

At the beginning of the ceremony, the flames can acquire even more meaning than unifying two lives. Parents and grandparents can pass a flame to their children as a symbol of family heritage and tradition. The wedding party can pass the flame as a symbol of friendship and support. Some ceremonies have tapers given to all the guests. By passing all of their flames to the new couple, the entire community is symbolizing their support. At the end, the couple joins their two flames together as one. Fire as it burns upward is always changing and renewing. As the flames are passed and used to illuminate the new relationship into which the bride and groom are fusing, the contradictory image of the candle's fire, at once delicate, ethereal, and elemental, beautifully sums up the paradoxes which are a part of all relationships. I always advise my clients not to extinguish their individual candle after lighting the unity flame. To be strong as a couple, they must remain strong individuals. To emphasize this concept, I usually end the lighting ritual by asking the couple to hold hands. Many cultures use binding as part of their marriage ritual. In the Philippines, a cord is tied around the couple's waist. In Hindu celebrations, a sacred red cord is laid upon the couple's wrists. In my favorite adaptation of this tying together, I ask the bride to take the groom's hands and look at them while I speak of the life experiences these hands will now share. I then reverse the hands, asking the groom to take his bride's hands while he considers their future life together.

Most ceremonies have photographers snapping away during these proceedings. When I design a ceremony, I think pictorially; the unity candle and the hands held in front of the three candles make for an iconic image that tells the story to the guest onlookers. While most professional photographers are discreet, I have occasionally been shocked by someone's aggressive behavior. They want to record every moment, and many couples are willing to adjust the moment for the captured image. This too is a result of merchandising and developing technology. Although wedding portraits were always popular, in the 20th Century, wedding day documentation became the accepted style as equipment became portable enough to leave the studio. In 1929, David Berns perfected a lightweight, high-speed, portable camera that he could use to take publication quality candid shots of celebrity gatherings. *Town and Country* commissioned him to do a wedding spread, and the fashion for a documentary of the wedding day was begun.

Modern Alchemy

In 1935, Henry Luce began publishing *Life Magazine*. Bridal shots of common people were often featured. During the same period, Hollywood studios began to routinely release public relations photos of their starlets in wedding gowns designed by their top costume designers — not because the girls were getting married, but because a slinky white gown was a glamorous homage to American womanhood. The great studio heads all had backgrounds in the garment business and appreciated the power of beautiful clothes. Everyone wanted to be glamorous and famous for a moment in time, and a photograph was proof of the special moment. When World War II sent men off to war, soldiers could pin photos of their own domestic starlets next to Betty Grable's legs.

After the war, the wedding industry began to create "the picture story" of the entire day, a story which harkened back to fairytale images. A common shot of the 1950s wedding album was the bride staring into a mirror. The imagery of looking for the future in the magic mirror became the first visual chapter of the bride's transformation into the princess. Prince Charming would soon arrive. Soon they would live happily ever after. The wedding album was often bound and packaged like a visual treasure chest protecting these precious memories, preserving the magic spell. The photographer became the alchemist making each moment into gold.

In fact, the commercial cultivation of the wedding day into magical moments does reflect the effects of a well-made ceremony. The sequence of the candle, the hand holding, the reading of special words is a transformative formula used in magic, alchemy, and religion all over the world. With this sequence, I could be describing a séance or a wizard's spell or a religious liturgy. However, the photographer is not the magician. The transformative story of the ceremony comes from the sharing of words and actions by the couple in front of their family and community. When staging a ceremony, I try to make it as visually and aurally accessible to the guests as possible. As a civil celebrant, I prefer to stand to the side and in front of the couple so that when they face me, they are facing out to the guests. The couple and the ritual space in which they say their vows should be open to their guests. By this same reasoning, I rarely stage a ceremony inside a garden gazebo or arch, preferring to have the couple stand at the edge with the structure as a frame, but not an obstruction.

In some ways, understanding the magic of a ceremony is like interpreting a dream. Every image in a dream relates back to the central figure. At a wedding, while different characters perform different actions and say different words, everything that takes place is really about the main characters, i.e. the bride and the groom. The procession brings the energy of the community into the personal circle of the bride and groom. The power of the flames pass to the bride and the groom, symbolizing and emotionally effecting the changes taking place in their lives. So it is, at this point, that the officiant or a reader, shares special words, a magic spell, that bind together the physical world with the spiritual world. I do not perform a religious ceremony, and I try to explain myself in concrete terms, but I cannot deny that there is an energy that happens in ceremonies that is more than the parts. I call this spiritual. It is a cathartic release of cultural memory and personal feeling. We cannot measure emotion or define feelings with scientific exactitude. Try looking up "love" in the dictionary and see how weak the words seem; but, having brought energy into the room through actions, the ceremony must state the spiritual change that has taken place to anchor the intangible into everyone's awareness. Many religious ceremonies use 1st Corinthians:

If I speak in the tongues[a] of men and of angels, but have not love, I am only a resounding gong or a clanging cymbal. If I have the gift of prophecy and can fathom all mysteries and all knowledge, and if I have a faith that can move mountains, but have not love, I am nothing. If I give all I possess to the poor and surrender my body to the flames,[b] but have not love, I gain nothing.

Love is patient, love is kind. It does not envy, it does not boast, it is not proud. 5It is not rude, it is not self-seeking, it is not easily angered, it keeps no record of wrongs. 6Love does not delight in evil but rejoices with the truth. 7It always protects, always trusts, always hopes, always perseveres.

Love never fails. But where there are prophecies, they will cease; where there are tongues, they will be stilled; where there is knowledge, it will pass away. For we know in part and we prophesy in part, but when perfection comes, the imperfect disappears. When I was a child, I talked like a child, I thought like a child, I reasoned like a child. When I became a man, I put childish ways behind me. Now we see but a poor reflection as in a mirror; then we shall see face to face. Now I know in part; then I shall know fully, even as I am fully known.

And now these three remain: faith, hope and love. But the greatest of these is love.

I have always found this passage in its totality difficult, confusing. If I do use it, I prefer a shortened contemporized version which I include in Chapter 10. I much prefer a medieval passage *On Love* by Thomas à Kempis:

Love is a mighty power, a great and complete good. Love alone lightens every burden, and makes rough places smooth. It bears every hardship as though it were nothing, and renders all bitterness sweet and acceptable. Nothing is sweeter than love, Nothing stronger, Nothing higher, Nothing wider, Nothing more pleasant, Nothing fuller or better in heaven or earth; for love is born of God. Love flies, runs and leaps for joy. It is free and unrestrained. Love knows no limits, but ardently transcends all bounds. Love feels no burden, takes no account of toil, attempts things beyond its strength. Love sees nothing as impossible, for it feels able to achieve all things. It is strange and effective, while those who lack love faint and fail. Love is not fickle and sentimental, nor is it intent on vanities. Like a living flame and a burning torch, it surges upward and surely surmounts every obstacle.

Or this passage from Robert Fulghum's *From Beginning to End: The Rituals of Our Lives*:

You have known each other…through the first glance of acquaintance to this moment of commitment. At some moment, you decided to marry. From that moment of yes, to this moment of Yes, indeed, you have been making promises and agreements in an informal way. All of those conversations that were held in a car, or over a meal, or on long walks — all those sentences that began with, "When we're married" and continued with "I will and you will and we will" — those late night talks that included "someday" and "somehow" and "maybe" — and all those promises that are unspoken matters of the heart. All these common things, and more, are the real process of wedding.

The symbolic vows that you are about to make are a way of saying to one another, "You know all those things that we've promised and hoped and dreamed — well, I meant it all, every word."…

Look at one another — remember this moment in time.

Before this moment you have been many things to one another — acquaintance, friend, companion, lover, dancing partner, and even teacher — for you have learned much from one another these past few years. Now you shall say a few words that will take you across a threshold of life, and things will never be quite the same between you.

For after these vows you shall say to the world —

This is my husband. This is my wife.

Tears and Laughter

The three passages seem to be trying to make the same point. The choice must ultimately be based on personal preference and one's connection to traditional text. In various ceremonies, I have used other passages from such diverse writers as Mark Twain and Celine Dion, depending on my clients' choices. The style and tone of the words become secondary. Some couples prefer a casual style, while others are formal. The most important consideration is the message that is conveyed to everyone, not only the couple, but also their guests. Too often couples discount the power of choosing the right words and fear asking someone to do a reading. Not everyone is willing to give a ceremony the concentration it deserves. Also, we make our feelings vulnerable when we include others, even our closest family, in these rituals; so we hesitate, but when the words and the reader and the moment combine, the magic is powerful.

A large part of choosing the right words is giving everyone permission to laugh and cry. So much of the Victorian wedding tradition, grounded as it is in dated conventions, corseted and buttoned in stiff clothing that we no longer wear except for such occasions, keeps us armored and withheld. The idea of spirituality and sacred moment seems to call forth formality and serious intention. Because awesome and regal images have become the packaging of the catering hall, everyone feels a bit serious and intimidated; but just as clothing has changed over the years, so have our attitudes. The Victorian stiff upper lip has been replaced by a freedom to express our true emotions. Even though moments of significance seem to call forth solemnity, a reading is the time to remember that tears and laughter are mixed as we celebrate any life passage. Have faith in your friends and family. However much they whisper or stutter, their saying the words you have chosen will convey the message of your ceremony. I often add a personal story about the bride and groom to give the assembled community permission to laugh. Everyone has a story about the first time they met, or the wedding proposal, or the disaster that turned into proof of love. The wedding ceremony is a time of inclusion. Don't be intimidated by convention. Share.

Why You Love

The conclusion of the wedding ceremony is the exchange of vows and the presentation of the ring. Double ring ceremonies only came fully into fashion during World War II as GIs married and put a golden link on their finger symbolizing the connection to their bride back home. A golden ring is a circle and eternal, but it is also part of a chain that connects and anchors. The ring ceremony is an ideal place to say something personal as part of your vows. These words will be a binding link. In many ceremonies, these words are made into a document that the wedding couple signs. I often follow that custom. Some of my clients have even put their unique vows out at the reception for all the guests to sign as witnesses. Many couples are intimidated by the prospect of writing vows, but a speech isn't necessary. A simple list of why you love the other person is sufficient to acknowledge the connection being forged by slipping a ring on each other's hand.

After the exchange of rings, the officiant pronounces the couple husband and wife. I like to present them for the first time as a couple. The linking of their names to each other completes the purpose of the ceremony. While custom dictates that the woman take on the man's name, many brides prefer to retain their name or hyphenate it. Dependence, independence, and interdependence are the themes of a wedding ceremony. The goal is to create a ceremony which balances the tension between the commercial, the traditional, and the personal. The nature of our culture is to sell packaged dreams, but the wedding ceremony is a moment to assert the personal preference of the couple. The bridal experts gain authority by intimidation. By insisting on your individual words and style, you can create a ceremony which is warm and inclusive, not eccentric, but your own.

The Great Story

The American wedding as observed today is a wonderful costume party, with the humanity of the event pushing through despite the trappings. Even more is possible, however, if the ceremony becomes the core event of the evening. Your guests should go home talking about the words that were said, the moments which connected them to their own lives, and the personal details and stories that made the ceremony feel as if it could only have been written for this bride and groom The word *spirit* comes from the Latin "to breathe." The definition of *spirit* is an animating or vital force held to give life. The joy which makes us dance in the streets, that truly makes us equal to any king or queen, is a spiritual experience. We exchange breath when we share a wine cup, when we say our vows, when we kiss. Our breath forms words which animate the gathering to the great story of life's continuity. The great joy and paradox of humanity is that everyone's story is different, and everyone's story is the same, and everyone loves to listen.

Don't be sold someone else's version of your story. Stand up as you are and speak the truth of your feelings. The perfect wedding is your own.

THE PERFECT WEDDING IS YOUR OWN

The word spirit comes from the Latin "to breathe." We exchange breath when we share a wine cup, when we say our vows, when we kiss.

Now you shall say a few words that will take you across the threshold of life, and things will never be quite the same between you. For after these vows you shall say to the world: This is my husband. This is my wife. ROBERT FULGHUM

*Blessed are we
for the gift of the
fruit of the vine,
the symbol of joy.*
JEWISH

You are thought, and I am sound. HINDU

*In that book which
is my memory/
On the first page that
is the chapter when
I first met you/
Appear the words …
Here begins a
new life.*

DANTE ALIGHIERI

May your joys
be as bright as
the morning,
your vows
of happiness
as numerous
as the stars
in the heavens,
and your troubles
but shadows
that fade in the
sunlight of love.

OLD ENGLISH
BLESSING

A marriage makes of two fractional lives a whole, gives to two purposeless lives a work, and doubles the strength of each to perform it. MARK TWAIN

Most of what I really need to know about how to live and what to do and how to be I learned in kindergarten. Share everything. Play fair. Don't hit people. Clean up your own mess. Say you're sorry when you hurt someone. Live a balanced life. When you go out in the world, watch out for traffic, hold hands, and stick together.

ROBERT FULGHUM

Chapter Four

TEN TIPS FOR WEDDING

On September 11, 2001, Ted had planned to hang around his apartment. He had a day off from the fire house, but when he heard the news that a plane had crashed into the World Trade Center, he knew his engine company would be called to the disaster. They would need every man, so he went, arriving shortly before the first tower fell. Standing in the street as the building collapsed, he saw the black cloud of destruction rolling toward him, and he began to run. He couldn't run fast enough. The smoke and debris overwhelmed the streets, enveloped him in darkness. He felt objects hurtling past him. The noise was like a locomotive rushing over him. The cloud hit him, swept around him, but he was not touched, not even a scratch.

Eighteen hours later, he returned to his apartment thinking, "I've got to live. After seeing so much death, I've got to live." The previous week, a buddy from his engine company had played a gag on Ted, signing him up with an Internet dating service. Now Ted went to his computer and began to look through the profiles of young women. He saw a photograph of Pam, an attractive woman hanging off a cliff while rock climbing. "She looks normal," Ted thought and sent her a message…Two years later, I officiated at their wedding.

Ted didn't want to have the 9/11 story told at his wedding ceremony. He didn't want to be a hero at his wedding. Rather, he saw the wedding as a celebration of life, of renewal.

1 YOU DON'T HAVE TO TELL ALL THE DETAILS OF YOUR STORY TO TELL YOUR STORY.

A wedding ceremony includes the guests by letting them connect their own stories to that of the couple. Sometimes, this is done through the use of universal ritual symbols: fire, wine, water, food, flowers. Sometimes the recognition of shared experiences is conveyed in readings from poetic text, scripture, or personal writings. Sometimes we tell the anecdotal details of courtship.

Ted and Pam were married in a garden with attendants wearing the uniforms of service — firemen, policemen, and medics. The guests may not have been able to verbalize the story they were seeing, but the emotional image was resonating within them as soon as the procession came down the aisle. Life is fragile, but those who face death understand the importance of celebrating life.

2 RITUAL USES COMMONLY HELD IMAGES TO INVEST POWER BEYOND THE EVERYDAY INTO THE MOMENT.

The groomsmen in uniform represented the history of those uniforms as well as their personal connection to the bride and groom. The garden became the fabled gardens of history and poetry, the magic place of perfection which in its season will pass, but in the moment recalls paradise and the grace of rebirth and renewal. The ceremony became a commitment to life by the physical choice of setting and dress. Staging is a part of ritual. Ritual is the first theater. Theater is not pretending, but reality taken to a heightened symbolic level.

CEREMONY EXAMPLE ONE:

On behalf of Ted and Pam, I welcome you to this beautiful garden.

Spring is a traditional season to marry, a life affirming season. Tonight, we share with Pam and Ted this season when their lives will change, when two will become one in a new pattern of life: "As two trees deeply rooted in separate plots of ground reach up and out, forming a miracle of lace against the heavens."

We have put our lives aside this evening to come here from all around the world to celebrate the wonder of Pam and Ted's love. Here, in the open air, our laughter and delight in their marriage will rise up into the infinite heavens; and, later tonight, while we feast and dance, the echoes of their vows will still be traveling on, and on, and on, into the infinity of time. Pam and Ted are pleased to have you witness their love and hope that in hearing their vows, you will think of the love you feel for each other.

Pam and Ted met in the fall of 2001, shortly after 9/11. Ted was working at Ground Zero, but life was too much with him to let that destruction cap his desire to reach out to the world. He saw a photo of Pam literally hanging off a cliff and he thought, "She seems like a normal, stable person."

Pam decided to date him because he seemed "straightforward" and had a nice, soft face, and he liked scuba diving. She even let him pick her up on the first date at her home because, when she heard his voice, she thought he seemed so trustworthy.

I think what they sensed in each other was an honesty of feeling and an openness to the adventures that life will bring.

Pam knew how special Ted was on the first date because he had brought his photos and art work to show her. Here was someone willing to share who he is.

Ted literally fell hard for Pam on their second date when he went down while ice skating. Pam stood over him and laughed. The bruise hurt for months, but Ted had begun to love Pam's confidence, her integrity, and her presence.

And so, like the flowers in this garden, love was planted and grew and blossomed. Pam thinks of Ted and says that she never thought about being with anyone else. He speaks of marrying her and thinks of the love of his own parents, and of his grandparents Thomas and Margaret Quealy who were married for 53 years.

Ted and Pam look at each other and see the end of this story in the classic phrase, "Together, they live happily ever after."

3 A CEREMONY THAT SPEAKS WITH TRUE EMOTION IS HEALING AND THAT MUCH MORE JOYFUL.

When a divorced or widowed person remarries, his or her life history is present whether he or she chooses to acknowledge the past or tries to ignore it. Therefore, I encourage my clients to celebrate the twists and turns of life.

CEREMONY EXAMPLE TWO:

Joni was on a girl's night out when she met Jim, the stranger sitting next to her at the bar. As she and her girlfriend commiserated about men, she turned to the innocent bystander. Poking at him, she said, "You're one of them. What do you think?"

"I think," he said, "it would be nice if you would consider having dinner with me some evening."

A moment like this becomes the core of the wedding — a remembrance of loneliness and a rejoicing in union. To support this story, we chose to do a candle-lighting ceremony. Many weddings incorporate candle lightings. Fire is one of the worldwide symbols of renewal. In this case, we wanted the candles to include everyone who had been a part of Joni and Jim's journey, so we asked Joni's teenage daughter and Jim's brother, who was his best man, to start the candle lighting, and pass the flame through all the rows of guests. Each guest had been given a candle on being seated. Now the flame spread across the rows until 150 candles burnt brightly. Finally, two special girlfriends came up to pass the flame to Joni and Jim. The bride and groom then lit a unity candle, and all the other fire was extinguished. A third girlfriend read a wonderful ee cummings poem:

i carry your heart with me (i carry it in my heart)

i carry your heart with me (i carry it in
my heart) i am never without it (anywhere
i go you go, my dear; and whatever is done
by only me is your doing, my darling)
i fear
no fate (for you are my fate, my sweet) i want
no world (for beautiful you are my world, my true)
and it's you are whatever a moon has always meant
and whatever a sun will always sing is you
here is the deepest secret nobody knows
(here is the root of the root and the bud of the bud
and the sky of the sky of a tree called life; which grows
higher than the soul can hope or mind can hide)
and this is the wonder that's keeping the stars apart

i carry your heart (i carry it in my heart)

In the visual beauty of the candle lighting and the casting of the girlfriends, Joni and Jim created a telling of their story. Everyone in the room witnessed the magic of the blessing that happens when two people meet and begin again. Everyone knew the past and saw in the unity candle the creation of the future. Everyone knew that they had been invited to be present because they were a part of the journey.

4 POETRY IS A FORM OF STORYTELLING WITH HEIGHTENED IMAGERY AND EMOTIONAL RESONANCE, SERVING MUCH THE SAME FUNCTION AS PRAYERS AND BLESSINGS IN A RELIGIOUS CEREMONY.

Joni chose this wonderful poem by Yevgeny Yevtushenko:

No, I'll not take the half

No, I'll not take the half,
Give me the whole sky! The far-flung earth!
Seas and rivers and mountain avalanches —
All these are mine! I'll accept no less!

No, life, you cannot woo me with a part.
Let it be all or nothing! I can shoulder that!
I don't want happiness by halves,
Nor is half of sorrow what I want.

Yet there's a pillow I would share,
Where gently pressed against a cheek,
Like a helpless star, a falling star,
A ring glimmers on a finger of your hand.

5 GREAT POETS HAVE GIVEN THEIR WORDS TO EXPRESSIONS OF RELIGIOUS RITUAL. DON'T BE AFRAID TO GO BACK TO IDEAS FROM YOUR TRADITION TO EXPRESS THE MIRACULOUS FEELINGS OF YOUR LOVE.

Norlyn and Ed met at a ballroom dance hall. (I profile them further in Chapter One) Norlyn, a widow, and Ed, a recent divorcee, used the classes as a method of "getting back out into the world." Both still held a great deal of pain from the past, but found their present and future much like a fairy tale. They are a modern Cinderfella and Cinderella. As in the classic story, their lives have been emotionally reduced to ashes until they experience transformation at the ball. The ritual core of this ceremony's story was dance — the dance of life — the patterns of dancing becoming a symbol of the dips and turns of life's journey. The ceremony took place in the dance hall where Norlyn and Ed had met. An 8,000 square foot ballroom with crystal chandeliers, the cavernous space might have dwarfed the wedding party; but instead, it became a spectacular setting for a culminating Viennese Waltz, performed by the newly married couple. We began with an invocation that echoed traditional Jewish wedding vows.

CEREMONY EXAMPLE THREE:

Norlyn and Ed have come to this moment from different sides of the world; but both of their traditions recognize that past, present, and future are all present when two souls pledge themselves to each other. In the Jewish tradition, this chuppah is the dome of heaven and a reminder of the temple of Solomon which stood where heaven and earth meet. When two souls who are meant for each other come together to wed, as they do tonight, heaven and earth meet and all creation rejoices. The Jews call such a moment B'shert.

6 SONG LYRICS ARE POETRY.

The ceremony continued with the evocation of Astaire and Rogers, dancers whose films have become icons of elegance and romance.

Norlyn and Edward, do you remember the movie *Top Hat*? Fred Astaire takes Ginger Rogers into his arms and sings:

Heaven, I'm in heaven
And my heart beats so that I can hardly speak
And I seem to find the happiness I seek
When we're out together dancing cheek to cheek

Dance with me! I want my arms about you
The charms about you
Will carry me through to...

Heaven... I'm in heaven
And I seem to find the happiness I seek
When we're out together dancing cheek to cheek

You are our Fred and Ginger, and even more romantic and glamorous than they, because your love is real. Ed, you told me Norlyn came to you like a gift, like a reward for being good. Norlyn, you told me that when you visited with Ed's family in Croatia, it was as if fate had brought you back to the soil from which you sprang. Ed and Norlyn, when you talk about dancing you both smile. Because it brings you joy. Norlyn, you told me that Ed is a very good lead. He told me that in dance, "A woman needs to be displayed." Certainly, when he took you in his arms, you knew that you were meant to be partners. It was a snowball dance. Ed turned to you and asked you to join him. He looked into your eyes, and you began to dance The Merengue. Soon after the first dance, Norlyn, you had to leave, but Ed followed you into the hall where you were changing shoes. He had to cool off. You spoke. You gave him a kiss on the cheek, and your business card. Heaven would soon have you dancing cheek to cheek.

7 THERE ARE NO WEDDING POLICE.

A wedding is a public declaration of who you are to each other, and your ceremony should reflect your personalities. Most of the traditions which we use in the modern wedding ceremony date from Victorian times. Just because Queen Victoria made it fashionable doesn't mean you have to follow her rules. Have fun with your wedding.

Tammy and Jeff met through a personal ad on the Internet. Jeff's ad told a story: "I'm walking down a street. I pass you." Tammy responded to the ad by finishing the story, "I pass you. I stop. I notice you." Obviously, they had to meet each other. Tammy told me that before she even met Jeff in person, she knew that he was different, to say the least, and that he would have to look like Quasi Moto for her not to like him. They went out on a date to see a movie, "Saving Private Ryan." You might think that a movie where everyone dies is not a great first date. But Steven Spielberg starts his movie with one of the most harrowing war sequences in cinema history. Tammy was grabbing hold and would not let go of Jeff for the first five minutes of the film. Jeff had a grin from ear to ear. Later, while driving in Tammy's "jacked-up" Bronco, Jeff said to her, "Let me see your hand." Tammy gave Jeff a weird look as if to say "why," and plopped her hand out to Jeff. He then took Tammy's hand in his and held it all the way home. A few weeks later Jeff gave Tammy a Turkish puzzle ring, and asked her to be his girlfriend. Tammy responded by punching Jeff! Tammy gave up cigarettes for Jeff, at which point Jeff knew he had met his mate. They say of each other, "She has everything I don't have." "He has everything I don't have." Together they have the world.

They planned to make their wedding vows on the front steps of a porch in suburban New Jersey. Fifty guests would sit in folding chairs on the lawn to witness the event. The wedding party would be modest, but they wanted vows that would be as filled with delight and surprise as their romance. They asked me to write vows that would echo Dr. Seuss. In general, I understand my job as a celebrant, as an interpreter of the clients' personalities and styles. I don't impose my taste when it comes to poetry choices or rituals. I offer suggestions and then make the clients' choice work. I trust that my clients and I will find a common ground; but this request took me somewhat aback. Vows in doggerel? "I could try," I said, "but I'm not sure it won't be too silly." The vows are a place in the ceremony when you want the gathering of guests to recognize the universality of the moment with words that echo generations of tradition. To me, Dr. Seuss didn't quite seem to fit, but I put my mind to it. One of the connections between Tammy and Jeff was their love of animals. Everyone knew they had four dogs and numerous other rodents, lizards, and birds. In their ceremony, I used an anecdote about a duck as a metaphor for their courtship.

CEREMONY EXAMPLE FOUR:

One day, Jeff was driving along Route 80 in his BMW, late, as usual, for work. He noticed four goslings by the side of the road, trembling in the shadow of an 18-wheeler. Now, you and I might have sped by at 65 miles per hour (which is exactly what Jeff did). But then, the little angel on his shoulder, Tammy, said "Jeff, you cannot leave those poor goslings. Go back and get them." Jeff decided that he *had* to go back and get the goslings, as Tammy would never forgive him. He had to travel another 5-10 miles to make a U-turn on Route 80, and then another 5-10 miles to come back and collect the goslings. So here is Jeff, on the side of Route 80 with cars flying by, collecting four goslings and putting them in the back of his BMW. Jeff got into the Beamer and began to drive, thinking, "What the hell am I going to do with these goslings?" As he was driving he noticed two adult geese and decided to bring one of the goslings over to them to see if they were the parents. Of course, the two geese flew away, wanting nothing to do with the gosling. Jeff scooped up the gosling, put it in the back of his car with the other three, and continued on his journey. Finally, he came upon a farm with a pond. He released all four goslings on their merry way, and there they are to this day, swimming away, hopefully forever after.

Here today, you, Tammy and Jeff, are embarking on a new cycle of life. Although you claim to be opposites who complement, in fact you are connected not just by your love for each other, but by the caring and attention you give to the world, and which make us who are assembled here today, your family and your friends, love you. We, as you did with the goslings, stand here to witness your release into the pond of life together, hopefully ever after.

Here, then, were all the images of Dr. Seuss: The journey down a high-speed road; the importance of finding a home in which to settle; soft and vulnerable animals. The vows suddenly wrote themselves (with thanks to the good Doctor, whose words have become American icons of playfulness and innocence).

GERRY:

Tammy, please look at Jeff and repeat after me.

Tam, I am. I am Tam.
Would you walk with me as the years do span?
Could you, would you, on a train?
Would you, could you, on a plane?
Will we, shall we, build our house,
With dogs, and ducks, and a small, soft mouse?
Will you marry me forever? Do you vow to love me?
Wherever, whatever?

JEFF:

I do.

GERRY:

Jeff, please repeat after me.

I am Jeff. Jeff, I am.
Will you marry me, dear Tam?
Would you, could you, on a train?
Could you, would you, on a plane?
Will we, shall we, build our house,
With dogs and ducks and a small, soft mouse?
Will you marry me forever? Do you vow to love me?
Wherever, whatever?

TAMMY:

I do.

8 MAKE SPACE FOR THOSE WHO LOVE YOU TO EXPRESS THEIR LOVE.

Many traditions have formulas for giving away the bride. This moment at the beginning of the ceremony can be one of the most meaningful moments for the entire family.

Lee had come to the U.S. as an immigrant from Malaysia. She had successfully started a hair-styling salon in Manhattan and was in her late 30s. One day, a customer suggested that her brother John, a confirmed bachelor in his 40s, might be a perfect match for Lee. A meeting was arranged, and the rest was history. Their story had an epoch quality. It encapsulated the hardships of immigration, the difficulties of finding a match in the big city, and the desire for both John and Lee to find a life partner after more than half a lifetime alone.

We decided to incorporate Lee and John's Chinese heritage into the wedding with a tea ceremony. We decorated the ceremonial space with a great bowl of oranges and a beautiful Chinese tea set. John's mother and all of his aunties would sit in the front row while the bride and groom served them tea. Each auntie would sip as a symbol of their acceptance of Lee into the family, and, as Chinese custom dictated, each auntie would then place a red envelope with good-luck money upon the tea tray. Based on a traditional ceremony, with ancient symbols, the sharing of tea highlighted the importance of family and old-world values; but we chose a sophisticated, contemporary reading from Pablo Neruda's *Ode to Common Things* as an accompanying text to bring this ceremony into the 21st Century. The lyrical words of one of the world's great living poets reminded us all that although aunties no longer rule over the new bride, the ties of family and memory make us who we are and have a place in every new household.

CEREMONY EXAMPLE FIVE:

Welcome to the wedding of John and Lee. Let us join together, as family and friends of the bride and groom, to celebrate and bless the beginning of their married life and the continuity of family. John and Lee have come to this moment from different sides of the world, but out of a similar tradition that recognizes that past, present, and future are all present when two souls pledge themselves to each other. This bowl of oranges, in the Chinese culture, symbolizes the good fortune and prosperity that lies before them.

But oranges are sweet and tart. Life and love are not a simple path. John and Lee have waited almost half a lifetime for their souls to meet. Death and distance prevent their fathers from witnessing this happy event. We honor them at this moment and ask the matriarchs of the family, as keeper of the family traditions, to accept and sip a cup of tea from Lee to symbolize the entry of this new couple into the Chow household and their gratitude to you their parent.

John's mother Pearl, Sio Chu Chow
and his aunts
Sio Lee Yuen
Sio Yu Wong
Sio Zea Wong
Cecilia Yih
Ms. Koo

(John carries the tray to the ladies, and Lee pours
a cup of tea for each lady, who takes a cup and sips)

Tea like love is common and complex. Pablo Neruda writes:

Tea like the heart
arrives bearing
stories,
thrills,
eyes
that held
fabulous petals in their gaze
and, also, yes,
that scent of Jasmine
and of dreams,
that scent of wandering spring.

9 THIS IS YOUR WEDDING. DON'T BE AFRAID TO BE PERSONAL IN THE CHOICES THAT YOU MAKE. THE GUESTS ARE THERE BECAUSE THEY LOVE YOU AND WILL FEEL HONORED THAT YOU HAVE FOUND A WAY TO SHARE THIS MOMENT WITH THEM.

Lisa and Eric met when Lisa was 23 and Eric was 16. (I profile them further in Chapter One) Needless to say, their relationship didn't take off, but they always stayed in touch. Eric's dream was to follow the Renaissance fairs across the country. Lisa wanted a grown-up relationship. It took 13 years. When Eric finally was ready to start his adult life, Lisa was still available. She hesitated and her mother said, "If you love him, be with him."

While we often think masculine energy is the dominant force in creating a couple (after all, the man proposes), the old folk tales recognize that the feminine is the path to wisdom and renewal. Lisa and Eric's lives paralleled the traditional formula whereby the man could only grow wise and come to his full self by recognizing his need for the woman. In order to tell their story, we decided to use a traditional Armenian tale.

CEREMONY EXAMPLE SIX:

There was a prince who spent his days in hunting and pleasure. Once, he lost his way in the mountains. At last, he found water and, parched, ran to drink; but as he bent down to the stream, he saw the reflection of a lovely woman standing over him.

"Here," she said, "Use my jug to drink and drink slowly. The water is too cold to be gulped." He looked at her and saw beauty and wisdom. He took her jug and drank deeply.

"Come with me to my father's house. You must be hungry," she said. And he followed her.

Although her father was only a shepherd, the house was filled with beautiful carpets which the girl had woven. The prince had never seen such beauty and, in truth, had never before taken the time to look. Overwhelmed with love for this talented and kind girl, he fell to his knee and asked her to marry him.

"Do you have a trade?" she asked.

"I'm a prince," he replied. "I don't need to know how to do anything."

And she laughed at him. "Don't you know that fate can tumble even the mightiest into the dust? When you have learned a practical craft, I will be your bride."

So the prince returned to his palace. He no longer spent his days hunting. Now he practiced weaving and knotting. The years passed, and from practice, the prince learned to make fine rugs. Finally, when the time was ripe, he took gold and silver thread and wove a rug of unsurpassed beauty. Then, straight away, he galloped into the mountains and found his love.

"Here," he said, "this rug is your wedding gift."

"Have you learned a practical trade yet?" she asked.

"This is my work," he said. "I have become a weaver of beauty like you."

And so the girl agreed to marry him. They ruled the kingdom together: He taught her to read books, and she taught him to read the hearts of men.

Lisa and Eric made unusual choices for the physical aspects of their wedding. Although I am a civil celebrant, they chose a wonderful church as the setting for their ceremony. Sacred does not have to be formally religious. Although intimate, the church space had a soaring wooden dome and lovely stained-glass windows. When the guests entered this graceful and beautiful space, they left their everyday world. Whether they were religious or not, the colors and warmth of the church's interior created a sense of the sublime. In commercial spaces, bookstores and theaters, the tradition of folk tales is often diluted into stories for children. In this sacred space, the use of the folk tale as parable became not just commentary on the lives of this couple, but a recognition of the commonality of all of our lives: a lesson in the patterns of courtship and the miracle of finding one's helpmate. This was sermonizing as the ancients might have done: teaching and celebrating our universal journey of life and recognizing a spiritual energy that cannot be named. Lisa chose to wear a brilliant red wedding gown. Passion and magic marked her entrance into the space as a classical guitarist played the processional. Everything was exceptional. Nothing could be taken for granted. This ceremony was a moment to be remembered for everyone present, not just for its beautiful images, but because it was truly the coming together of the young couple, the end of the old story and the beginning of the future for Eric and Lisa.

10 MOST PEOPLE TAKE THEIR LIVES FOR GRANTED, BUT WHEN YOU TELL YOUR STORY, YOU DISCOVER THAT THE ORDINARY CONTAINS THE EXTRAORDINARY.

Todd and Michele met in college. They were both active in theater and part of a group of theater people who regularly worked and played together. But it took a semester before Michele managed to meet Todd after a cast party for "The Three Sisters". That's when she confessed to two girlfriends that she had a crush on Todd. They squealed that he was one of their best friends, and they loved him, and they loved her, and YES the two of them should meet. *So was that that?* Noooo. Although their extraordinary chemistry became apparent immediately, things were a "little messy." Just because you're dealt the cards, doesn't mean you know how to play them. Todd was seeing someone else. It would be months before he and Michele began to see each other. *So was that that?* Noooo! Shortly after he and Michele began to see each other, he panicked and told her he couldn't continue with their relationship. She did what any sensible person would do. She took her broken heart out into the pouring rain, got into her car, and sobbed. And then, in the midst of her cries came a tapping. Todd was at the window. He got into the car, held her hand, they kissed, and all wounds were healed. *So was that that?* Nope. Then Michele dumped Todd for another guy, until she realized what she had thrown away.

So it went for 10 years.

Until they were both invited to a friend's out-of-town wedding. Michele at that point had resigned herself to being alone forever. Todd was in a serious relationship. But, when he and Michelle were in a room together this time, the chemistry was inevitable. They got a glimpse of their future together. Todd recognized that they had been dealt a royal flush. Three weeks later, back home, Todd called Michele with big news. He had broken up with his girlfriend with the express intent of getting back together with Michele. Michele's response? "Okay. . .but what now?"

Michele had, for her part, been feeling the same feelings as Todd, but assumed she'd have to wait until after his other relationship had run its course. So, Todd's news came as a shock. She wasn't prepared to get what she wanted so soon. Todd, sensing this, acknowledged, "It's hard to be noncommittal when you get back together after a decade." From that day on, Todd and Michele have, in a sense, been exchanging vows every day. To quote Billy Crystal in "When Harry Met Sally," "When you realize you want to spend the rest of your life with somebody, you want the rest of your life to start as soon as possible."

Todd and Michelle wanted to tell their story at their wedding with humor, sentiment, and style. They wanted to acknowledge that you can be dealt your cards, but you have to know how to play them. They designed a deck of cards to give to each of the wedding guests as a favor. I explained:

CEREMONY EXAMPLE SEVEN:

When I count the number of spots on a deck of cards, I find 365, the number of days in a year. There are 52 cards, the number of weeks in a year. There are 4 suits, the number of weeks in a month. There are 12 picture cards, the number of months in a year. There are 13 tricks, the number of weeks in a quarter. In this favor are all the days of our lives. How we play them is up to us. We celebrate that you two in taking your vows tonight have been dealt a full house.

Todd and Michele's theatrical connections helped us continue the numerical theme of counting our days. We chose a song from Jonathan Lawson's Broadway show "Rent," and asked one of Todd and Michele's theater friends to sing "Season of Love":

525,600 minutes, 525,000 moments so dear.
525,600 minutes — how do you measure, measure a year?
In daylights, in sunsets, in midnights, in cups of coffee.
In inches, in miles, in laughter, in strife.
In 525,600 minutes — how do you measure a year in the life?
How about love? How about love? How about love?
Measure in Love. Seasons of Love.

Michele's grandfather had recently died, and she wanted to acknowledge this loss. A moment of memory is not an uncommon request; and in this case, I felt it even reinforced the couple's story of loss and restoration.

Last father's day, Michele and Todd went to Michele's grandfather's bedside to have their rings blessed by Father Jack, his parish priest. They had announced their engagement at his 90th birthday party; and now as he lay dying, they wanted to give him, a deeply religious man, the gift of witnessing the blessing of their union. Michele and Todd did this for Grandpa Martorana, but it was also an engagement present to themselves; for it served as a powerful reminder of what it means to love, and what it means to truly be a part of a family. Tom Martorana died on June 21. Let us remember him, and let us remember Kathleen Carlstrom, Todd's grandmother, who died last winter.

The ancients told time by the moon, whose phases singled not only the passage of days, but also the changing of seasons. Todd and Michele's journey into each other's arms had many seasons; and, at last, on their wedding night, a full moon shone forth in all its glory and engulfed everyone in a magical light. Like the waxing and waning of the moon, our lives change and sometimes feel diminished by sorrow and loss; and yet, always the hope of tomorrow, the knowledge of a new beginning, lies in the mystery of our darkest hours. Everyone loves a wedding because a wedding is a reminder of hope, a universal human moment which declares we are here now. Whatever was is past, and we, out of the power of our love for each other, start over. I blessed Michele and Todd with a lyric by Paul Kelly from "Mushroom Music":

I have the moon in my bed.
Every night down she falls.
I have the moon in my bed,
I had nothing, now I have it all;
And I have the sun in my heart,
When I rise by her side.
I have the sun in my heart,
Even through the darkest night.
She can save me from myself,
Make me feel like someone else,
When I hardly know myself,
I have the moon in my bed,
I have the sun in my heart,
I have the stars at my feet,
I have the moon in my bed.

The moon, the sun, and the stars are the most common elements of human life, and the most extraordinary when truly considered. When making your wedding, look to the truth of your life together and the ordinary miracles which you will now share. Who could ask for more as a blessing on their wedding night!

Chapter Five
DEALING WITH FAMILY

A Jewish folk tale tells of a rich man who held a great banquet to celebrate his daughter's wedding. As was the custom, everyone in the town was invited and all came. In the midst of the festivities, there was a knock on the door. The rich man went to see who was still out on the street and discovered a beggar in rags. "Come in then," said the rich man. "Sit in a corner and have something to eat." "Oh no," said the beggar. "I wish to be like all the other guests. To sit and eat and dance with the bride." "What,!" shouted the rich man, "You near my daughter? How dare you even suggest such a thing. Throw him out!" And the rich man's servants tossed the beggar back out into the road.

A few minutes later, there was another knock at the door. The rich man went again to see who it could be. This time he saw a stranger dressed in a fine suit. "Come in, come in," said the rich man. "All are welcome in my house. Please, traveler, sit in a place of honor by my daughter the bride. Eat and drink." The stranger entered and sat. Food was brought and wine was poured; but when the meat was put in front of him, the stranger took it with his hands and rubbed it on his shirt. He stuffed his pockets with the salad and poured the wine into his top hat. "What are you doing?' cried the rich man. "What behavior is this?" The stranger replied, "When I came before in rags, you turned me away, but when I came in fine clothes, you treated me with honor. Obviously it is my suit and not me that is invited to this feast. So it is my suit and not me that should eat." With that the stranger disappeared into the air, and everyone realized they had been visited by the Prophet Elijah, testing the goodness of their hearts.

A Generous Gesture

One of the greatest problems of a wedding is whether to include unpleasant guests with whom we are estranged or who, simply put, will bring additional stress to the day. Many young couples have parents who have divorced and remarried. What to do with the extra wives and husbands? There is nothing worse than divorced parents behaving badly. I think wedding couples have to protect themselves if they know that a stepparent or estranged parent is going to become a nightmare at the ceremony. On the other hand, I believe a generous gesture can sometimes change our lives, and a wedding often brings the best out in people. We never know when the blessings of the Prophet Elijah will come dressed in rags.

Often the issue comes down to who gives the bride away.

Rosemarie's mother and father were divorced, and her father was estranged. In addition, Rosemarie's mother had remarried and become a Jehovah's Witness and would be offended at any sense of religiosity. Rosemarie wanted a secular ceremony, but with the traditional and heartfelt sense of occasion that ritual brings to a life event. She wanted to be walked down the aisle by a male member of her family, and to have her mother participate within the ceremony as a mark of her caring and nurturing; but she didn't want her stepfather to give her away. Brides often want a father to give them away even if their closer attachment is to their mothers. What to do? Often, I point out that brides do not have to choose, but can walk down the aisle solo. However, this solution takes a confidence that most of us do not feel at that wonderfully vulnerable and meaningful moment when our lives change. Instead, we constructed a ceremony so that everyone was made to feel special. We would acknowledge the parents for the happiness they bring to the wedding couple, but redefine their role in the ceremony. We decided to have Rosemarie's grandfather be her escort as a mark of honor and respect. To reinforce the concept of generations, we included a moment at the ceremony's beginning to remember the grandparents who hadn't survived to experience this happy day. We then asked the mothers to give their children away by reading poems of advice and blessing which they had chosen for the occasion.

CEREMONY EXAMPLE EIGHT:

Tonight, we stand here with Rosemarie and Ron to witness their union, and to offer our love and support for their future life together. Recognizing that love endures in joy and sadness, that life brings both bitter and sweet, we remember Ron's grandparents Gloria and Louis Petrone and Alice Matthews, wishing that their lives had lasted to bring them to participate in this moment of happiness; and we rejoice that friends and family have come here tonight, despite distance and years, to see and hear the vows that Rosemarie and Ron will offer each other.

I ask Ron and Rosemarie's mothers to give their children to each other by reading two poems.

CAROL:

When you are married, you join hands and become one.
As you walk through life together,
remember that you are unique,
and different from one another.
Give your love openly and honestly.
Do not try to change each other –
your differences helped to bring you together.
Always respect and accept what the other has to say,
even if you do not agree.
And most importantly, remember that
you are two separate and special individuals.

Take time to enjoy every day you share together
and remember that each day is a new beginning.
You will be sharing todays and tomorrows
together, and making each one more treasured
and more complete than anyone could make alone.
A marriage is a home, interwoven with hopes,
memories, and dreams.
The thankfulness and love it can bring have no comparison.
In marriage, walk the path together,
side by side whenever possible, and remember
to hold each other when it is cold.
If the air becomes too close,
make a little space so each can breathe.
When the path is narrow, pick one to go first.
Be willing to follow and never be afraid to lead.
Trust your partner; trust yourself,
for marriage is a journey that leads to great love.

LUCILLE:

Apache Wedding Prayer
Now you will feel no rain,
For each of you will be shelter to the other.
Now you will feel no cold,
For each of you will be warmth to the other.
Now there is no more loneliness,
For each of you will be companion to the other.
Now you are two bodies,
But there is only one life before you.
Go now to your dwelling place
To enter into the days of your togetherness
And may your days be good and long upon the earth.

How to include extra stepparents is often an awkward problem. The easiest and most controllable way, while still acknowledging the birth-parents, is by giving these stepparents a special time to enter, just before the procession, but after all the other guests have been seated. As they take their places in the front row, the ceremony begins. The processional pattern can then include (1) the birth-mother and -father coming in together either as a couple, (2) or separately with a close family member escorting the mother, and the father escorting the bride, (3) or mother and father both escorting the bride. The procession is a wonderful moment in the ceremony. It provides a physical image of everyone's support of the new couple. Don't trivialize it because of the tension of family dynamics. Use it as a generous gesture of love and respect by asking people to be involved. Be creative with it. Find diplomatic permutations of order and seating to smooth over emotional agendas and preconceptions.

Box Seats

When Alyson and Jose fell in love, their Jewish/Cuban union caused parental stress. In the Jewish tradition, both sets of parents walk their respective children down the aisle and stand with them during the ceremony. Alyson's mother secretly phoned me to ask that Jewish ritual be followed for the procession. Jose and his family called wanting a blessing by a priest who was a family friend. Adding to the confusion was this reality: They all loved each other despite their different cultures and religions. The bride and groom finally came to me. They wanted to avoid any issue by cutting ritual out of the occasion. They were opting to have a wedding party, but with as little ceremony as possible. "Short and sweet" was the expression.

Weddings should be happy occasions. Of course, some nervous anticipation might be unavoidable, but one way to minimize the stress is by sticking to what's familiar. Amazingly, ritual follows familiar patterns across cultures. An anemic wedding ceremony will feel awkward and empty to everyone. The solution of doing nothing will never be satisfactory. Instead, the common patterns need to be highlighted and redefined. First, we needed to talk through the procession. Everyone felt comfortable with having the parents in the procession and the bride flanked by her parents. We reconfigured the seating pattern of usual flat rows, so that special chairs would be placed on either side of the ceremonial space, essentially creating box seats for the parents who could stand or sit after entry and still be present with the bridal party. Jose's parents led the procession. Jose followed them with his best man. The groomsmen and bridesmaids came next, with the maid of honor finishing the entrance of the bridal party. Then, to a new musical theme, the bride entered with her parents flanking her. While Jose stepped forward to lead her to the officiant, every one remained standing. I then asked the guests to sit, and called the parents up from their special places to give their children to each other. We incorporated the Jewish symbol of the bridal canopy or *chuppah* with a hand-binding ceremony that is adapted from the Catholic Church.

CEREMONY EXAMPLE NINE:

Let us, family and friends of the bride and groom, join together this morning to celebrate and bless the beginning of Alyson and Jose's married life, and the continuity of their two families. There is a Yiddish expression, B'shert, which means fated, ordained in heaven. Alyson and Jose come to this moment from different traditions; but both of their traditions recognize that past, present, and future are all present when two souls pledge themselves to each other. In this beautiful garden, we stand beneath this bower of flowers called a chuppah. In the Jewish tradition, this chuppah is the dome of heaven and a reminder of the temple of Solomon which stood where heaven and earth meet. When two souls who are B'shert come together to wed, as they do tonight, heaven and earth meet and all creation rejoices. Rob and Debbie, Pedro and Josepha, please stand with me as we give your children to each other.

The parents stand behind their children as Gerry reads.

Jose, please take Alyson's hands and hold them palms up in yours,
so you may see the gift they are to you.

These are the hands, young and vibrant with love that reach out to you
on your wedding day as she gives you her pledge and accepts your ring.
These are the hands that will hold you in joy, excitement and hope.
These are the hands that will hold your children in tender love, soothing
their hurts and wringing themselves with worry when trouble comes.

These are the hands that will hold your face and wipe tears from your eyes, the hands that will comfort you and hold you when fear or grief rack your mind. These are the hands that will touch you in wonder and awe that you would cry for her. These are the hands that will caress you for a lifetime. These hands are smooth and young and carefree now, but will be lined and rougher when years go by. Still they will reach out to touch you with their love, and you will reach out to hold them.

Alyson, hold Jose's hands in yours, palms up, so you may see the gift they are to you. These are the hands, young and strong and vibrant with love, that hold yours on your wedding day as he promises to love you all the days of his life. These are the hands that will hold you in joy, excitement and hope. These are the hands that will be so gentle as he holds your baby for the first time. These are the hands that will comfort you in illness and hold you when fear and pain rack your mind. These are the hands that will touch you in wonder and awe that you would cry for him. These are the hands that will caress you for a lifetime. These hands are smooth and young and carefree now but will be lined and rougher when years go by. Still, they will reach out to touch you with their love, and you will reach out to hold them.

Alyson and Jose, please clasp hands. These are the hands that will enter a life together. These four hands will be your armor and shield. They will reach out to each other and, then united, spread your love and caring to all they touch.

These four hands will build a home of love and sharing.
You may release your hands.

In the Hispanic tradition, the bride and groom ask a couple to stand as the godparents of their wedding, to guide them through the ceremony and to continue to support them throughout their lives. We entwined this concept with the Jewish tradition of a Ketubah or marriage contract. The procession over, both set of birth-parents sat in their special seats, while the godparents or *padrinos* were called up. Alyson and Jose's parents had given them away; the padrinos would be the guides into the new relationship of marriage. Alyson had searched the Internet and found a site that specialized in calligraphy and design of ketubahs. This beautiful decorated document was on an easel during the ceremony and then at the reception, displaying the wedding vows at the heart of the occasion. It would make a lovely piece of art to hang in Alyson and Jose's new home as a memento of their wedding. Now the bride and groom signed their promises to each other, and the officiant and the padrinos signed as witnesses. To cover the time it took for all of this, Adelo, the close family friend who was a priest, read in English and Spanish from the Old Testament Song of Solomon, one of the most sensual and beautiful of all Biblical books.

Adelo reads in Spanish.

ADELO:
Cantares 2:8-10,14,16;8:6-7a

8¡Ya viene mi amado!
¡Ya escucho su voz!
Viene saltando sobre los montes,
viene saltando por las Colinas.

9 Mi amado es como un venado:
como un venado pequeZo.
¡Aquí está ya, tras la puerta,
asomándose a la ventana,
espiando a través de la reja!

10 Mi amado me dijo:
"Levántate, amor mío;
anda, cariZo, vamos.

14 "Paloma mía, que te escondes en las rocas,
en altos y escabrosos escondites,
déjame ver tu rostro,
déjame escuchar tu voz.
¡Es tan agradable el verte!
¡Es tan dulce el escucharte!"

16 Mi amado es mío, y yo soy suya.
Él apacienta sus rebaZos entre las rosas.

6 Llévame grabada en tu corazón,
¡llévame grabada en tu brazo!
El amore es inquebrantable como la muerte;
la pasión, inflexible como el sepulcro.
¡El fuego ardiente del amor
es una llama divina!

7a El agua de todos los mares
no podría apagar el amor;
tampoco los ríos podrían extinguirlo.

From the Old Testament, The Song of Solomon 2:8-10, 14, 16; 8:6-7a

I hear the voice of the one I love, as he comes leaping over mountains and hills like a deer or a gazelle.

Now he stands outside our wall, looking through the window and speaking to me.

My darling I love you! You are my dove hiding among the rocks on the side of a cliff.

Let me see how lovely you are! Let me hear the sound of your melodious voice.

My darling, I am yours, and you are mine, as you feed your sheep among the lilies.

Always keep me in your heart and wear this bracelet to remember me by.

The passion of love bursting into flame is more powerful than death, stronger than the grave. Love cannot be drowned by oceans or floods.

Waters from the Four Corners of the World

Anjalee's mother was dreaming of a big wedding for her only daughter. Anjalee is south Asian from New York, and Terry is a southern Californian. When they met and fell in love, they proceeded to embark on a transcontinental courtship. Not only did they live on opposite ends of the continent, but their cultures came from opposite ends of the earth. Their wedding would be attended by Anjalee's family from Asia, Africa, Europe, and North America. Terry's family was a bit overwhelmed by the energy and elaborate customs of Anjalee's Indian culture and wanted a western ceremony. Like many of my clients, Anjalee and Terry's first impulse was to minimalize ritual and have a short ceremony that would primarily be the marriage vows. However, their instinct told them that they and their guests who had come so far would feel cheated. My job was to create a wedding that would not only formalize this union, but also welcome and acknowledge the guests who had traveled so far to see the young couple enter a new life together. Furthermore, I felt it was fitting to honor the bride's mother for whom this moment was so important.

The image of journey was so strong in this story. I suggested we create a ritual to memorialize the distant places from which family had come. With the invitation, we sent a request for vials of water from the major rivers and seas by which guests lived. The waters were placed with a crystal bowl by the ceremonial space. After the procession had entered, we created an invocation, a calling together, that echoed Hindu prayer by combining the waters while blessing the four directions of love:

CEREMONY EXAMPLE TEN:

We gather today to celebrate the love and union of Anjalee and Terence, who bring to each other the unique treasures of their families and their traditions as they create a new household. Their destiny was to find each other, across oceans and continents, propelled by love. We come here from the four corners of the world as witnesses to this love. We have been asked to bring water, the source of life, from the oceans and rivers that flow through the many lands which this love unites, so that we may combine them here. From the sacred Ganges, from the Indian Ocean, from the Pacific, from the Atlantic. As these waters flow together, let the blessings of all of our traditions flow upon this loving couple.

Gerry pours the vials of water into one bowl as he says

The sacred east — where the flaming sun arises
Let your love be a light and inspiration to yourselves and to the world.
May all your mornings be blessed with love.
The sacred south — where the earth offers her abundance
Let your love support your planting and harvesting,
both as individuals and as a couple.
May all your days be blessed with love.
The sacred west- where the noble sun sets
Let your love be a comfort to all your disappointments,
a mirror to all your hopes.
May all your nights be blessed with love.
The sacred north — where the soul's compass finds its home
Let your love be a guide to your passion and powers and your progress in the world
May all your years be blessed with love.
These four corners of the world are the sacred directions of love —
May you be held within their center — Now and for the rest of your life together
for a long time to come! And may all your dreams come true!

I then incorporated a flower presentation to the bride's mother, honoring her before all her guests.

Each member of the wedding party is carrying an orchid as a symbol of your love. Orchids grow on air and seem to create their delicate beauty as if from nothing. In truth, the great forests in which they grow protect and nourish them with a mighty canopy. Anjalee's mother Sudah Warrier has nurtured and protected both of you; and these flowers, which symbolize love, are given to her as thanks for the unconditional support she has offered as you leave her household to create your own.

Melissa, please gather the orchids.

Gerry gives Anjalee and Terry a flat tray to hold as Melissa gathers the blossoms and places them on the tray. Gerry binds the orchids into a bouquet. Melissa gives Mrs. Warrier the bouquet.

Traditional motifs of flowers, water, and poetry made everyone feel that they were seeing something familiar and heartfelt.

True Love is a Sacred Flame

Alysha and Chris had four sets of parents in attendance, which wasn't as much of a problem for the bride and groom as for the various stepparents who didn't have good relations. We wanted the birth-parents to be involved with the ceremony, but they needed to be kept separate. Tension was high enough that we wanted them to be equally involved, equally honored, and quickly sent back to their spouses so that the ceremony could move beyond the recrimination of the parents' relationship and celebrate the real emotional core of the ceremony, the optimism and commitment of the young couple. We decided to make the unity candle do double duty as a symbol of reconciliation of family as well as union for the bride and groom. We found a candelabra that held five flames. First, both birth-fathers, and then both birth-mothers were called to light a taper and, with its flame, light one of the candles on the candelabra. Then the children took the flame from their parents and lit the final candle. The groom's sister read a poem, "True Love is a Sacred Flame," while all the assembled guests witnessed the beautiful picture of both families holding burning tapers, reconciled in this moment of support for the children who were about to start their independent life journey.

CEREMONY EXAMPLE ELEVEN:

We light a flame to symbolize the love that has nurtured Alysha and Christopher and brought them to this moment. Barry Schwartz and Mark Day, please come up and light a candle, for it is your love that shaped the individuals that Alysha and Christopher are today.

They come up and light candles and stand next to the bride and groom.

Sheri Schwartz and Diane Comet, please come up and light a candle, for it is your love that gave your children life, teaching them the love and caring they now give to each other.

The mothers come up and, taking a candle, light it off of the father's flame and stand beside their children.

Alysha and Christopher, will you each light a candle and then light this one candle with both your flames. Today, two become one. May love burn in you always.

Sarah Day has a poem to share with you:

SARAH:

True love is a sacred flame
That burns eternally,
And none can dim its special glow
Or change its destiny. True love speaks in tender tones
And hears with gentle ear.
True love gives with open heart
And true love conquers fear.
True love makes no harsh demands
It neither rules nor binds,
And true love holds with gentle hands
The hearts that it entwines.

A New Life Together

Ben and Amelia are a May-December romance with an almost 40-year age difference between husband and wife. Ben's children were not happy with their father's choice. As he put it, they told him he was nuts. Who can say what circumstances will make a happy union, or how love is sustained. There is no foreseeing the future, and a celebrant is not a therapist. More than half of American marriages end in divorce. My job was not to take sides, but to bring everyone together to celebrate the moment. Fear is always present at a wedding. The new couple, no matter how well they know each other, or how long they have been together, is heading into a new relationship with a much deeper commitment. A ceremony must acknowledge this fear and state the responsibilities and conditions of the marriage contract. By law, the officiant must warn the couple clearly and simply: Their public agreement to their union is entered into with all intentions of it lasting for life. Traditional ritual creates marriage vows and contract signings as well as literal hand-tying to symbolize this binding agreement. Marriage is "for better or worse, to love and honor and protect." In the case of Ben and Amelia, I wanted to express the many emotional and life considerations of the relationship without sentimentality, and as straightforwardly as possible, so everyone could hear. Mark Twain gave me the words to lead into the wedding vows:

CEREMONY EXAMPLE TWELVE:

A marriage makes of two fractional lives a whole,
gives to two purposeless lives a work,
and doubles the strength of each to perform it;
It gives two questioning natures
a reason for living and something to live for.
It will give a new gladness to the sunshine,
a new fragrance to the flowers,
a new health to the earth.

Did I satisfy Ben's children? No, but I used the ceremony to truly tell the story of the couple's relationship. This started their marriage with words that empowered their unique commitment, and stated publicly the complex considerations which push lives in new directions.

No one can say what lies around the next bend, but the words of a ceremony illuminate the next step of two lives becoming one. Fear and excitement are a part of starting over; and fear and excitement can provide the impetus for moving forward more aware, more alive, and more committed to a new life together.

Chapter Six

PARTNERSHIP –
THREE COUPLES'
HEART OF WEDDING

There is an Old Testament teaching about the name of God which is never spoken. In Hebrew, the name of God is spelled with four unaspirated consonants: No sound. Hebrew does not include written vowels. So no one knows how the name of God would sound if spoken. Supposedly, the only time any one did speak the Ineffable Name was on the holiest day of the year. The high priest would enter the Holy of Holies in the center of the Temple of Solomon in Jerusalem, the center of the world. There, the priest would stand alone before God and utter His name. What were the sounds of this sacred utterance? If one were to take the letters that we have and try to speak them, all that comes forth is breath; just as it is said that God breathed into Adam to make life in the divine image. Perhaps there is nothing missing or lost from the biblical transcription. Perhaps breath is the sound of God's name and image? And life, therefore, is a constant prayer praising the name of the creator?

I cannot understand the reasoning of any religious person who would deny the fullness of life to another of God's creatures. Love, children, growing old with a partner and a family, these are basic experiences for humanity and part of the divine right imparted with God's breath. Just as I cannot support that there is only one way to marry, so I cannot support that the state of marriage is exclusive to some people and not to others. I am horrified by the debate pushed forward in the United States by the religious right that same-sex couples should not have a marriage recognized by the state. Surely, a church has its right to define its own beliefs. But surely, in a civil society based upon the concept that all men are created equal, all citizens should have the right to celebrate the miracle of life and love by marrying someone with the intention of sharing the rest of their lives together. God did not give the word *marriage* to Moses on Mt. Sinai. The religious do not own the concept of marriage. Rather, our civil government gives religious groups the right to authorize unions that will then be recognized by the state.

Marriage in the United States is a local issue. Each state has its own set of laws, although there is reciprocity between states. I can meet someone on Monday, go to Las Vegas on Tuesday, and marry my new love on Wednesday, without worrying that New York State may challenge my commitment to my partner — except if my partner is someone of the same gender. So it is, that I can marry someone I have known for only 72 hours, but I cannot marry someone with whom I have lived for a decade and with whom I intend to live for the rest of my life. Until such time as the federal government is willing to trump the states and invoke the equal protection clause of the 14th Amendment, gay and lesbian couples are not protected by U.S. law.

Since stable family relations are an asset to any society, shouldn't we use the word marriage for all permanent unions, civil and religious, and encourage the emotional and financial stability which marriage supports? In a heterogeneous society, how can we justify distinctions and prohibitions based on orthodox Abrahamic religious traditions? The state does not sanctify marriage. The state encourages and records marriage so that property and civil and health rights can be protected. In a modern society, there is no ethical, practical, or emotional benefit to denying a basic human right to any group of citizens.

Pioneers

Alice and Hazel (I use pseudonyms because they fear discrimination at the work place if their story is known) decided to get married after a 10-year relationship. They will be wed with a civil union certificate. "We're the first of our friends, the pioneers," they say. "We have friends who get rings, go away to someplace friendly like Provincetown to exchange them, and that's the end of it." Many of their friends have discounted the advantages of civil unions because "state rights mean very little. Without the federal government behind it, a marriage between a same-sex couple means very little." Why didn't Alice and Hazel do the same?

They recognize that a wedding is not only a celebration, but also a moment of transformation, a psychological turning point as well as a public declaration. Hazel says, "The best way to define it is our parent's stairwell. That stairwell has pictures of the entire family. They have pictures of their step-grandchildren who have their boyfriends and now husbands up there, and we're not up there. The minute we get married, and we have a professional wedding, that ceremony will be up there on that wall. They're not ashamed, but there's a difference. The minute we get married, it will be different."

In fact, their parents have "been on their backs" for years, saying, "Come on, when are you going to tie the knot?" Their families want the best for their children and have long ago recognized the bond which connects their daughters, but choosing to have a same-sex wedding demands courage, even with a supportive family and in a state that recognizes civil unions.

"The location we've chosen for the ceremony has a restaurant with a big glass window. Lots of people will be looking. I know some folks will be shocked to see two brides in wedding gowns," Alice says. "It's going to be an incredibly long time before it is unacceptable to be discriminatory against gays and lesbians. It's just passively accepted. I work for a government institution, and our equal-employment administrator says 'fag' in a derogatory way, and everyone accepts it. I never forget that. So, on some level I do not feel accepted. I feel it's important, even aside from all the legal benefits it may bring — which are few and far between — to tell people we are good enough. We're not that different when it comes right down to it. We are as legitimate a couple as anyone getting married, and we are going to do what you do. We deserve it, and that's another reason I want to do it. It definitely will make people think twice."

Alice and Hazel don't see themselves as confrontational people, but by the nature of our society, they understand that their choice to ask friends and family to witness their connection to each other challenges the dominant cultural preconceptions of the wedding ceremony. Hazel tells this story: "My nephew Cody, my sister's son, is blind and autistic. He is mainstreamed in a local public school which prides itself on its inclusivity. Recently, the children were asked to list why they felt grateful. Cody, he listed his family including his aunts and uncles ending with Aunt Alice and Aunt Hazel. 'Who are they married to?' The teacher asked. 'They're Aunt Alice and Aunt Hazel,' Cody replied. 'But where are their husbands?' The teacher was insistent that Cody understand that women need men. 'They don't have husbands. They have each other,'" was Cody's knowledgeable reply.

Cody stuck to his guns. He knew Aunt Alice and Aunt Hazel belonged together. That day, the school sent home a note, worried about Cody's confusion. The teachers were so shut in by their own restrictive thinking that they never considered that Cody was telling the truth. In fact, he clearly understood what the authorities could not conceive. He had always received love from these two partners and, in his narrow world, saw the fundamental emotional truth of their nurturing relationship to him and to each other. His teachers were not anti-gay; they were culturally impaired and could not see.

The ties of marriage, despite the protestations of the conservative religious, have never been solely gender dependent. From ancient times, marriage has been based on a variety of practical issues including property, division of labor, and social status. In our modern era, immigration and residency, health insurance and estate planning, trophy wives and political and business acumen, all become part of the rationale for a marriage. Yet, most states will refuse to issue a license to same-sex couples that want to have society acknowledge their commitment to each other. Our laws are culturally impaired.

At their fifth anniversary, Hazel and Alice felt that the time had come to deepen their commitment. They wanted a ritual to mark the emotional progress of their lives. They went to a jeweler to purchase commitment rings. Alice explains, "It was a sign to society that I love you and you love me. I pledge myself to you." At this moment in their lives, if they had been a straight couple, they might have gotten married or at least announced their engagement. As a same-sex couple, they didn't have these options. New Jersey did not yet offer civil unions. Nevertheless, they decided to exchange and wear the rings on their right hands until they could, in fact, be married; but modern life is too complicated to be neutral.

They had created a private ritual, but we all have public lives. When you try to live without telling, people want to know. Clients and coworkers asked "Are you married?" to which they would reply, "No, not yet." "Isn't that a wedding ring," the questioner would insist. "No, not yet." was the reply. "What's his name," was the friendly follow up, to which they would have to reply, "I'm sorry. I keep my outside life outside my work." While many of their coworkers might not care, the reality of their jobs is that their career advancement will be affected if they acknowledge the fact of their partnership. Without active malice, the majority culture expresses prejudice through small indignities which unwittingly dehumanize the person to whom we are speaking. When critics of gay marriage urge "don't ask, don't tell" they are asking people like Alice and Hazel to hide and sacrifice the reality of their humanity.

Alice and Hazel sadly accept that the federal government denies them the benefits of a married couple, but they want their relationship to be as emotionally full as any other marriage. Five years after buying their commitment rings, they have made the decision to turn them into wedding rings. Part of the process of our becoming couples comes from how we are viewed by our community. Alice and Hazel decided that they wanted their 10-year anniversary to reflect the maturation of their relationship. They wanted to have another ritual. Since their first exchange of rings, their home state of New Jersey had legalized civil unions, and they wanted to express their connection in front of the family and friends who had supported them for a decade. As she thinks about her upcoming ceremony, Hazel says, "A legal document can't say this is who you are emotionally. You're not tied to it, but if you have the ceremony in front of other people, it is more of a commitment. I think it creates a statement. You take it more seriously and work harder."

Alice and Hazel see this wedding as a threshold event in their lives together, a crossing over into a new status. "You are making the announcement that your priorities are changing," Hazel explains. "My primary family is now my spouse. When you are growing up, your primary family are your parents and your siblings and, now, you're saying this is my family, this is my primary family." Hazel decided to propose at the same local restaurant in which they had their first date. The restaurant was very excited and helpful and arranged to seat them at the same table at which they had sat 10 years before. Hazel bought a more formal ring with stones to give Alice, and had it hidden in the menu that the hostess would bring to them after they were seated. Usually a marriage proposal will ripple through a restaurant, eliciting congratulations and toasts, but a woman kneeling before her partner, or two women holding hands and kissing across the table, is a dangerous image in a public forum. The actual moment of proposal was quiet and discreet. They reached across the table to each other and voiced a simple "yes" lest anyone attack them in the midst of this meaningful and intimate moment.

But for Alice and Hazel, their decision to hold a wedding ceremony gives them the opportunity to be open and excited about who they are and how much they love each other. They plan to arrive at their wedding by boat with a bagpiper leading the procession up from the dock. There is a Shelley poem titled "Love's Philosophy" which will greet their arrival:

The Fountains mingle with the river
And the rivers with the ocean,
The winds of heaven mix for ever
With a sweet emotion;
Nothing in the world is single,
All things by a law divine
In one another's being mingle —
Why not I with thine?

See the mountains kiss high heaven
And the waves clasp one another;
No sister-flower would be forgiven
If it disdain'd its brother:
And the sunlight clasps the earth,
And the moonbeams kiss the sea —
What are all these kissings worth,
If thou kiss not me?

I will escort them from the dock to stand in front of their supportive and protective family and community. They will openly and loudly say their vows, and I will proclaim, "I now pronounce you married in our eyes."

A Feast from the Table of Life

My friends Scott and Wallace have had a 30-year marriage in all but legal terms. New York State does not grant marriage licenses to same-sex couples. They are registered as cohabitating partners in New York City in order to qualify for the legal benefits that the city then guarantees by law. This, however, does not give them equal rights with married couples, but it gives them more rights than if they did not register; and these rights only apply in New York City. An hour's drive north from New York City, Connecticut recognizes same-sex marriage, but, of course, in this case there is no reciprocity between states. Therefore, although the option is available, Scott says this option is a sham until such time as his relationship is legally recognized in his own place of residence, i.e. New York City. Thirty geographical miles means the difference between inclusion and exclusion. The federal government would not tolerate such exclusionary practices for any other category of person, but, in this case has supported discrimination through the Defense of Marriage Act. Scott and Wallace are lucky. As professional, urban Americans, they have the means and knowledge to adjust for the shortfall of legal rights which their home state denies them; but what of the emotional rights which marriage entails? How does one protect them?

To Scott, marriage is more than a government registry; it is recognition by the community of the connection he feels to Wallace. Scott says, "I want people to look at me and know that I am married, that I am committed to Wallace." Thus, he demonstrates the stability of his connection to his life partner through his life choices. Thirty years ago, when he and Wallace had dated for some time, he said (as any heterosexual partner might have said), "If we are going to be serious, we have to live together." As New York City stories often go, he had the better apartment, and as New York stories go, both men had career opportunities which almost immediately pulled them apart; but they had made the commitment — home was always together back in Brooklyn. As in all committed relationships, the hardship of working out of town was meliorated by the support of a partner who could provide encouragement through good and bad times, and help look into the distant future. When Scott and Wallace are asked about their lives together, they both recognize that their relationship has supported and strengthened their professional as well as their personal growth.

For their 15th anniversary, they planned a trip to Amsterdam. At that time, jewelry stores in their Greenwich Village neighborhood had begun to sell "commitment rings" for gay couples. Scott wanted to exchange rings as a symbol of their connection to each other. He wanted a ring that everyone could see, a relationship that everyone could see. They bought a pair of gold bands and took them along to the Netherlands. There, they exchanged rings over dinner, a ritual spoken in a soft voice. Upon returning to New York, Scott felt himself self-consciously touching and playing with his ring. He realized he was more vulnerable because of it; that anyone at any time might now ask if he was married or say, "I didn't know you were married." Suddenly, the impulse to recognize his relationship with Wallace had become a public statement of his right to value his same-sex relationship with the same weight as any straight couple would give to their relationship. While Scott was not in the closet, he suddenly realized that his ring was an open announcement to the entire world that his love had as much worth as anyone's.

The truth of a simple personal ritual had become a public act with enormous personal and political symbolism. That was in 1996. Today, although the state has not yet gained the courage to register same-sex marriages, storekeepers in Greenwich Village now call the set of rings they sell to same-sex couples "wedding rings." Language is important; as more couples insist on calling their relationships marriage, and as the straight culture sees these partnerships legitimized by practice and ceremony within their own extended families, friends, and co-workers, I am sure that discrimination against gay and lesbian couples will disappear, and a more tolerant generation of Americans will take control of their society. But that time will only come as gay and lesbian couples willingly show their commitment despite the fear of disapproval and discrimination. Pioneers need courage to advance into a new landscape. Celebrants need to help chart the way.

For their 25th anniversary, Scott and Wallace planned a party at their home in Woodstock, New York. They invited the friends and family who had been important to them through all their years together to come and celebrate their long relationship. I suggested that they have a ceremony to mark the occasion. Not a marriage ceremony (for they still don't have access to a ceremony that conveys legal recognition), but a ceremony of community recognition, a marking of the past, a celebration of the present, and a wish for the future. We had enjoyed many a time cooking together, and I suggested that we create a feast of life to serve to their guests as a metaphor for the ceremony.

There are four tastes: sweet, sour, salt, and bitter. Each flavor contributes to the complexity of a dish, and complements the totality of the experience that is a beautiful meal. So it is with life. Marriage is a complex journey, and a ceremony to celebrate a marriage must reflect that complexity. An ancient Jewish custom is to break a glass at the end of the wedding ceremony. No one knows exactly why. Some say as a reminder of the fragility of human ties; some say as an echo of the glasses that rowdy guests will break against the wall in celebration. Life holds contradictions. Scott and Wallace's complex journey demanded a full taste of life, peppered with the mixed recognition that even life's heartbreak and fragility had added to the zest of this celebration. Together they had dealt with the death of family and close friends, cared for each other through major illnesses, supported each other under the pressures of career changes, and shared the rewards of love and friendship that had created a gracious home and a deeply caring community.

A CELEBRATION OF 25 YEARS OF COMMITMENT
SCOTT C. AND WALLACE N.
JANUARY 21, 2006
LAKE HILL, NEW YORK

GERRY:

Good afternoon, I am Gerald Fierst, civil celebrant. On behalf of Scott and Wallace, I welcome you to this celebration of their 25th anniversary and invite you to feast upon the flavors and memories which have sustained and nourished their commitment to each other as friends, lovers, and life partners, now and in the future. They invite you to add your memories and wishes to the guest book on the front table. Our love for them increases the pleasure of today.

I have prepared a little plate of memories from the table of life and ask them to taste a pickle. **Sour is a flavor that accents and highlights.** In the beginning, starting out in Park Slope, there were separations as Wallace went off to do nine months of stock and Scott worked as company manager at Northshore Music Theater. Scott had given up a job in New York at the Youth Symphony to go to Massachusetts, looking to gain an opening into the world of theatrical producing.

Wallace encouraged him to go even though it meant being apart, as Scott encouraged Wallace to take classes and train his voice as a singer. Wallace auditioned and went off for jobs.

That's what you do when you are young and together. Large separations accent the bonds; Rent is paid by temp work. Ironing boards are your desk. When they were forced to move to Washington Heights, Scott turned the sour separation into a money-making advantage, subletting the empty bedroom to roommates while he slept under the piano. You made the sour into the adventure of life and love. When there was a need to do something, you found a way to do it.

Here is a taste of Artichoke, a savory reminder of how Wallace's family embraced Scott. Wally, Wallace's father, would drive from Yonkers and pick them up in Washington Heights to bring them to holiday meals. Scott first tasted artichokes at Wallace's mother's table. Food is love. Gloria and Wallace's two sisters had given them a food processor to celebrate their first apartment together. Gloria's love for Wallace embraced and nourished them both. Scott loved the big Italian American feasts. He loved the family Wallace brought to them as a couple. He loved being a family with Wallace.

Here is radicchio. How bitter was the loss when Gloria died so quickly of cancer so soon after Wallace's sister Suzie's death after a long fight with leukemia. The long and difficult illnesses of Dan Michaud and of Wallace's Aunt Rose also took beloved people from Scott and Wallace.

But your love for each other has sustained your connection to them and to each other, and has strengthened the connection that you two make as a family, as it did just recently when you both had major surgery. You do what you need to do, in careers, in life.

Here is a salty olive. The French say a meal without salt is like a beautiful woman with only one eye. You have filled your lives together with a world of creativity and connection. Music is the salt of your lives. Music brought you together. Scott was working at the Little Opera Company and Wallace was working with Lou Rogers — which brought them to a conference where they had ended up meeting and having lunch together. "Gee, we should get together again sometime," they both said, and New York being New York, they never did. Then a month later, Dame Janet Baker was performing at Carnegie Hall. Wallace bought box seats for himself and his mother. A board member from the Little Opera Company gave Scott a ticket to a box. And so they ended up sitting in the next box from each other. "This is too bizarre," they laughed, "we should get together sometime." At the intermission, Scott got his coat from the anteroom. Wallace went to get his coat. It was gone. "I think that's my coat", Wallace politely observed to Scott. They had identical coats, and Scott had taken the coat from the wrong hook. Their first date was a cabaret performance at Jan Wahlman's.

Here is some sweet wine for the two of you to share. Wine is a traditional element in ceremonies. Wine is transformational. A magical brew made from common juice. Barrow Street and Woodstock, your homes and lives transformed with the brew of the fringe, the ballet, the theater, artwork, painting and singing. The ferment of your lives, careers and friends, transforming two lives into one home. I ask you to sip from this common glass, sharing breath as these sips represent shared lives. We kiss as a symbol of the sharing that love brings, of the connection that love transforms into a lifetime of experiences and feelings. Sip by sip, lip to lip, with this wine, you acknowledge your mutual sharing of joy and sorrow. Together you sip, may your joys be doubled; together you sip, may your sorrows be halved. Together you sip from the cup of life. May the wine always be sweet.

Scott and Wallace sip

As we all savor this moment, I ask us all to taste one of the olives we have been given and enjoy the sweetness of this moment as we wish Scott and Wallace:

May all that you are, always be in love.
May all that is love, always be in you.
May your love be as beautiful on each day you share,
as it is on this day of celebration;
and may each day you share be as precious to you as the day you first fell in love.
May you always see and encourage the best in each other.
May the challenges life brings your way make your connection even stronger,
and may you always be each other's best friend and greatest love.

Wallace's sister Sandy has some words to read:

Sandy reads.

On behalf of Scott and Wallace we invite you all to feast upon this table of love.

At dessert, we serve Champagne. Amy proposes a toast.

One Hundred Per Cent On Board

Chris and Leah became engaged while vacationing in Hawaii. Leah had already bought a ring planning to propose; but on that fateful day Chris was flipping through a magazine and casually said, "I was thinking maybe while we are here, we should go to a justice of the peace and get a civil union." "Well," said Leah, "if we are going to do it, let's do it right and have all our family and friends there."

Here is the choice so many same-sex couples must face:. To accept the circumscribed rights assigned to them within the confines of another state's legal system, or to create a ritual at home that may not have any legal power but offers the potential of emotional truth.

Chris says she wasn't anxious to have an inclusive ceremony unless everyone "was 100% on board." She had been to other ceremonies that "felt a little bit hokey and sad" because they were pretending to be a wedding when too many of the guests doubted the legitimacy of the ceremony. When Leah suggested this alternate plan, Chris felt that Leah was putting off a commitment by suggesting an event which wasn't real. Later in the day, however, while walking on the beach, Leah pulled out a ring and proposed, and Chris said yes; but what did yes mean? In fact, two committed people had very different concepts of how to celebrate their deepening attachment. The exchange of a ring to Chris was a statement of long-term commitment — a binding — but she did not need a public recognition of her attachment to Leah. Rather, it was a personal demonstration that she and Leah could now plan the "building of a family as a unit." Leah, a minister in the United Church of Christ, felt the exchange of the ring was first step of a sequence which begins with a private moment and ends with a public ceremony. As she said, "Marriage is a huge blessing."

The day of their proposal, Chris called home to tell her mother that Leah had given her a ring. "That's cute," her mother replied. "How's the weather." While accepting that her daughter had a same-sex partner, the idea of a same-sex wedding could not even be verbalized. After they returned home, Chris went to visit her family. "Want to see the ring?" she asked. "Why would you have a wedding?" was the reply. Chris's father kept repeating, "But it's not legal. I read in the newspaper, it's not legal."

I think it is shameful that so many liberal and progressive politicians have pragmatically sacrificed marriage equality to avoid creating a debate that might hurt their personal and political agendas. When the law treats the life of our son or daughter, our cousin or friend, our neighbor or co-worker as less than a full citizen, one must begin to wonder about the integrity of our courts and legislatures. In the United States, gay men and women wanting to marry are routinely treated as lesser. Luckily, in a handful of states, courts and legislatures have responded to the right to marriage equality. For Chris and Leah, the impossible soon became normal. In October 2006, the New Jersey Supreme Court ordered the state legislature to give equal marriage rights to same-sex couples. By December, the legislature had responded with a bill establishing civil unions.

When Chris's father read the news that day, he excitedly called her to say, "Congratulations. I heard it is legal now." Chris says she never imagined that the legal and social acceptance of same-sex marriage would cause such a rapid emotional turn about. Leadership does make a difference. Suddenly Chris realized, "Wow, this is a big deal," for a private act had become a political statement. Her mother began to point out photos of Ellen DeGeneres on the cover of People Magazine. Within their community, they too were taking a risk to set an example. Their ceremony would be a precedent for many people.

Chris began to feel that she wanted this wedding to be no different than the wedding her parents would have thrown for her if she had been marrying a man. Leah felt the need to be married within her faith community. She wanted to make her vows before God as well as the community. Many people in the church wanted to contain the sense of union by calling it a commitment ceremony or a holy union. Chris and Leah had to lead forums on marriage equality to help congregants understand that the vows they would be making had the equal weight of the vows of any other couple who had stood upon the altar to marry. Leah explained, "These words were going to define the rest of our lives. It's how we see ourselves. To say we are civilly united doesn't make sense." The invitations used the words wedding and marriage.

When the day arrived, the congregation filled the church in support. Chris saw that her parents were surprised by the attendance and that the ceremony was celebrated on the main altar. She observed, "It's one thing to say,' it's okay, go ahead do it,' but I never expected the level of welcoming. Everyone came out."

Ceremonies give permission to feel a depth of emotion we cannot always sustain in the mundane world. Ceremonies are important for the observer as well as the celebrator. Chris and Leah's decision to marry was also a transformational experience for their community, as all weddings should be. Setting their ceremony within a tradi-tional framework validated the ceremony far more than any law could do. When Chris's mother came up to the altar to read 1 Corinthians 13, she began to cry. Her voice grew empowered, and she felt the full spirit of the moment — in her words "God was moving her" — and so she pronounced:

> *Love is patient, love is kind and is not jealous; love does not brag and is not*
> *arrogant, does not act unbecomingly; it does not seek its own, is not provoked,*
> *does not take into account a wrong suffered, does not rejoice in unrighteousness,*
> *but rejoices with the truth; bears all things, believes all things, hopes all things,*
> *endures all things. Love never fails; but if there are gifts of prophecy, they will be*
> *done away; if there are tongues, they will cease; if there is knowledge, it will be*
> *done away. For we know in part and we prophesy in part; but when the perfect*
> *comes, the partial will be done away. When I was a child, I used to speak like*
> *a child, think like a child, reason like a child; when I became a man, I did away*
> *with childish things. For now we see in a mirror dimly, but then face to face; now*
> *I know in part, but then I will know fully just as I also have been fully known.*
> *But now faith, hope, love, abide these three; but the greatest of these is love.*

As a civil celebrant, I am not anti-religious; I am inclusive. As a civil celebrant, I believe that society is bettered by giving all couples the choice to have life-passage cer-emonies that represent them fully — emotionally, legally, and culturally. Therefore, I find it hurtful that same-sex couples may be denied the support of their religious community. While many couples would not be comfortable on the altar of a church, and many fami-lies would not feel validated by the physical setting of an altar, if it is in your tradition, the ceremonies and rituals of religion carry power that inform the meaning of the moment for everyone. You must be true to yourself and to your guests.

Chris and Leah chose a second reading for their ceremony, Matthew: 22: "'My friend, how is it that you came in here without a wedding robe?'" The minister offered a homily based on this passage which admitted that not everyone present had originally been comfortable with a wedding between two brides. Not everyone will choose to come to a wedding when invited, and some come reluctantly without the proper attitude. Hopefully, as more and more people see the courage and caring of the gay and lesbian community, and as gay and lesbian couples use the words "marriage" and "wedding" with the full intention of their meaning, change will happen. American society's mean-spirited attitude will change. As Leah observed to me, "The more models that come forward of a higher level of commitment, the more couples will see themselves in that kind of relationship."

The Day Will Come

I believe the day will come when bigotry will disappear and a new generation of Americans will join Canada, Mexico, and most of Europe in recognizing the right of all citizens to have legal protection in long-term relationships. As more couples come forward to announce their commitment to each other, as our neighbors and co-workers no longer feel compelled to remain discreetly silent, and as our leaders on all levels of community speak out, the truth of our human commonality will supplant the fear of our differences. As each of us gets to attend the wedding of a gay or lesbian friend or relative, the network of support and acceptance will broaden. It all begins with two souls willing to say "I do."

Chapter Seven

RECOMMITMENT CEREMONIES: MAKING THE OLD WORDS NEW

HOW DO I LOVE THEE? LET ME COUNT THE WAYS.

How do I love thee? Let me count the ways.
I love thee to the depth and breadth and height
My soul can reach, when feeling out of sight
For the ends of Being and ideal Grace.
I love thee to the level of every day's
Most quiet need, by sun and candle-light.
I love thee freely, as men strive for Right;
I love thee purely, as they turn from Praise.
I love thee with a passion put to use
In my old griefs, and with my childhood's faith.
I love thee with a love I seemed to lose
With my lost saints. I love thee with the breath,
Smiles, tears, of all my life; and, if God choose,
I shall but love thee better after death.

—ELIZABETH BARRETT BROWNING

The Second Act

When young couples start to tell me their story, they will often begin with the statement, "We were friends before we got together as a couple. So it was easy, once we became a couple, because we already liked each other and knew about each other." I often think these are the couples whose marriages will flourish — as if anyone can foresee the future. Consider that half the marriages in America, including those sanctified by religion, end in divorce. Some marriages break apart early with the realization of misconceptions. Some marriages fail as midlife brings self-evaluation and adjusted expectations. Some marriages are presented with crises that change us until we are unable to sustain what was and have no ability to make something new. Some marriages make do and stagnate in regret. Life's journey is not a straight line. A marriage is inevitably an evolving relationship as years go by, offering tests and transformations with all the adventure, intimacy, and pain that change can bring. Even the best friendships will be strained, but in marriage, one's friend becomes one's life partner, sharing the journey and providing an intimacy acknowledged and supported by family, friends, and community. Thus, when we reach a point in the journey where we can joyously acknowledge a good partner and friend, shouldn't we celebrate the success of a life well traveled together with as much or more enthusiasm as we celebrated the beginning of the journey?

To some, a recommitment ceremony may seem sentimental, an overblown valentine. I have come to understand a recommitment ceremony as more. If after 10, 20, 30, 40, 50, or 60 years, a couple decides to restate their vows, I consider this ceremony as much a life passage event as the original wedding. I don't think of the ceremony as a nostalgic renewal of the old vows, but as a realistic acknowledgement of the challenges overcome, of the changes and experiences shared and of the commitment that continues to grow. So, a recommitment ceremony can include a fuller range of experiences to reflect the breadth of life contained within the marriage. It can include a remembrance of old vows, and it can also include a hopeful promise of continuing growth. It gives the couple, their family, and their friends a time to look back and appreciate (an important act in itself), but it also presents to all present a time to consider the passion and friendship with which the future will be lived.

When my wife's sister and brother-in-law, Sandy and PJ, came and asked if I would lead their recommitment ceremony, they had been married 15 years. They decided not to wait for a milestone anniversary in old age. They had both had major health issues in recent years. Coming out on the other side, they decided that they should celebrate the now. While sentiment made them want to repeat much of their original ceremony, they weren't interested in going down memory lane. They wanted to emphasize that the greatest rewards of their shared life together was the energy and support the years gave to their much anticipated future. PJ's daughter Kathleen Benedetti Fisher wrote a poem for the ceremony as a gift for them.

With These Rings

I

At my father's first house
there was a tree for me, a crabapple.

At the next house
he planted a row of seedlings
that raced us growing up.

At the next house
a severed pine provided sanctuary
for secrets like spin the bottle
and burials of birds.

After four children had gone
he planted a golden chain tree
in the front lawn.

II

The great transformers,
trees make soil from sand
even while most of a tree is dead
with just a living center,

The maps of their lives
recorded by rings.

When they share the weathering,
share rings.

III

We move, like trees,
from decade to decade, mostly asleep
with a faint heartbeat

Until something stirs us saying:
"I recognize you —
I know that weathering!
A season I thought only I knew.
*But there **was** you."*

IV

Saplings don't do well
when crowded
or when a sucker
is not pruned.

With one nip
the snipped shoot
restores the life
to the tree tips,
but what to nip…

They knew this.
They pruned.

They pruned some of it
over these years
with you.

V

Trees need their feet
in the ground
to withstand
whatever weather,
maybe, one year, a dying mother,
They can grow to lean together.

Trees do well with loving keepers.
When those tented wormy creatures
that feed on the tender parts,
multiply and don't know when to stop,
gorging themselves until a city of tents
threatens the trunk,
the nurserymen is there
just in time
with a brave hand
saying, "It's okay"
and take the city of tents away.

VI

With mirror-like harmony
like the fugue of genders

they broke eggshells
and filled the woods with noise.

The great transformers,
they made the marriage contract fit.

They taught us how
to vow equanimity and forgiveness.

She rested on him like a carpet of pine needles.
He covered her like a blanket of pine needles.

They took each other for granted
here and there
but they didn't fret.

Did they sit upside down in a recliner and holler?
Did they balance naked on one foot in a hammock?

I can't say, but
there was something
they knew.

They pruned.
They tended
They watered
They grew alone
They grew together.

This was an evolution
of their souls.

And again
with the living ring
they vow again

They wed.

In the symbol of the tree, Kathleen captured beautifully and uniquely the sense of time, growth and change that marriage brings. Imperceptible in the moment, the passage of time is marked in the tree by the rings that internally record the changing of the seasons. Sandy and PJ told me, "We wanted to state publicly, for our family and friends, that we hadn't forgotten what we said 15 years ago, that we are still in love with each other, that our marriage is still solid, and that we are still learning things about each other, still growing, and still living each day one day at a time."

Too often, the wedding culture only celebrates youth, taking the lead from the commercial merchandising of beauty, fashion, and style. Rarely do we take time to celebrate the experience and value of living. The highlight of the ceremony for Sandy was seeing the line of grandchildren come forward to present flowers. At their first wedding, PJ had six grandchildren. Now, there were 11, including a teenage granddaughter who had recently been adopted. Johnny, the oldest, had been the ring bearer at their wedding and now was present with his new wife. Public ceremonies are a time for inclusion, and, in their ceremony, Sandy and PJ celebrated the physical reality of their family's growth. "They were all so beautiful," Sandy said. "Even the boys were beautiful." The procession of children presented a testament to the history that had become this couple's shared life, with each grandchild representing a connection between the past and the future. Our romantic vision of a couple walking hand-in-hand into the sunset is only a part of the story. In truth, the wholeness of life includes times of looking inward, but also times of looking outward and forward. A recommitment ceremony makes time for both.

At their first wedding, PJ's daughter Maria played the flute. Now, Maria and her son Paul played a duet. Every member of the immediate family participated in this ceremony from baking and distributing heart-shaped cookies, to offering flowers, to sharing a reading, a toast, or a song. PJ notes, "It was a whole new generation coming up. We were acknowledged by all the grandchildren, and we said to them that we had made the right choice the first time, and our choice was even more right this second time."

Our market culture emphasizes immediate gratification and replacement of the old with the new. A recommitment of vows emphasizes the patience of growth and the cycles of the natural world. The ceremony began with words from "I Have the Moon in My Bed" by Paul Kelly and the Messengers. The extravagant lyricism of this song seems of another time. I have always thought of it as a medieval dawn song, sung by two lovers to capture the expansive power of their love. All the heavens are held in the marriage bed, and each soul is the entire world. When young couples feel these emotions, they are filled with passion and a sense of a unique love. When an older couple says these words, however, there is the wisdom of constancy and universality. The lyrics, "Even through the darkest night/She can save me from myself/Make me feel like someone else/When I hardly know myself" take on a new poignancy and power when age acknowledges the turmoil and loss that life brings. Acknowledging that a marriage can sustain itself "even in the darkest night" is a special lesson to be passed from generation to generation.

Sandy and PJ wanted to use the same marriage vows as when they married 15 years before. I suggested that we also ask the guests and families to acknowledge their connection to the couple. In both cases, the words took on resonance from everyone's shared history. First, I asked Sandy and PJ if they wished to go forward in marriage.

"Of all the men and women you know, you have chosen each other as life partners. Knowing what you know of each other and trusting in what you do not yet know, are you ready to go forward in marriage?"

I asked for a commitment to move into the future, not to restate the past.

They replied "We are."

I then asked the gathering for their affirmation of support.

"It is appropriate that you, the family and friends, are here to participate in this wedding. The ideals, the understanding, and the mutual respect which these two bring to this marriage have roots in the love, friendship, and guidance which you have provided them. Do you intend to continue with this support, please answer, "We do." "

They all heartily replied, "We do!"

Sandy and PJ's original wedding words now took on a special power.

"I want to live with you just as you are. I choose you above all others to share my life with me. I want to love you for yourself in the hope that you will become all that you can be. I promise to honor this pledge as long as life and faith endure."

This vow balances acknowledgement of knowing and accepting the other person "just as you are," but also that years and age have and will change us, but we will strive to be all we "can be." Sandy and PJ have woven a small ceremony into their daily lives. At some moment of the day, one stops and says to the other, "I do." The words are a continuing ritual affirmation of the vows they made to each other, and of the active energy which they promised to commit to their future together. While speaking to Sandy and PJ, they said the first act of their marriage had been really successful, and now they were starting the second act. "What will you do for the third act?" I asked. "Well, I think of most plays as being two acts," Sandy replied. A play is divided into acts not because of the need for an intermission, but because of a great change in the action. I would not be surprised if Sandy and PJ did celebrate a third act at their 25th anniversary. Change will come, and in their commitment to each other they will discover a new life together, even in old age.

THE RECOMMITMENT CEREMONY
OF RUTH ANN (SANDY) AND PJ B
JUNE 14, 2008

Musicians play. Gerry enters. Music stops.

GERRY:

Good afternoon, I am Gerald Fierst, a civil celebrant, and Sandy and PJ's brother in law. On their behalf, I welcome you to the renewal of their wedding vows. Before we begin the ceremony, please remember to check your cell phones.

The folklore says that all the angels in heaven laugh when two souls who are meant for each other meet. And so today we join the angels to laugh and dance and sing with joy that Sandy and PJ found each other from the many men and women of this earth, and in each other found all the joy of heaven.

I read a lyric from Paul Kelly and the Messengers:

I have the moon in my bed
Every night down she falls
I have the moon in my bed
I had nothing, now I have it all
And I have the sun in my heart
When I rise by her side
I have the sun in my heart
Even through the darkest night
She can save me from myself
Make me feel like someone else
When I hardly know myself
I have the moon in my bed
I have the sun in my heart
I have the stars at my feet
I have the moon in my bed

Music begins and grandchildren enter surrounding Sandy and PJ
and throwing flowers. Sandy and PJ come and stand by Gerry.

June is a traditional season to celebrate love, a life affirming time. As the leaves turn green and the flower buds open, you have asked us all here today to witness that you remain committed to each other through sickness and health, good times and bad, finding in your marriage the renewal of love so that every day you say to each other, "I do."

Around the world, ceremonies celebrate love by sharing something sweet. Mark has made a cookie for each of us to taste, so that we may enjoy the sweetness of this moment. Please take a cookie and hold it for a few moments. We will use it later for a toast.

Mark comes forward and tray of cookies is passed as musicians play Pachelbel Canon in D.

Sandy and PJ, please hold hands for a moment and look at each other.

May all that you are, always be in love.
May all that is love, always be in you.
May your love be as beautiful on each day you share, as it is on this day of celebration; and may each day you share be as precious to you as the day you first fell in love.
May you always see and encourage the best in each other.
May the challenges life brings your way make your connection even stronger, and may you always be each other's best friend and greatest love.

Each of your grandchildren has a stem of orchids to give you. Orchids seem to grow on air, but in truth they are supported by the full forest canopy beneath them. So, each of us is here because of a deep connection to you, and each of us stands here in support of your lives together and the future you will share. I call:

Music plays

Names of grandchildren
Kellie
Jonnie
Laura
Paul
Joe
Hannah
Chrissie
Dominique
Rachel
Lilly
Michael

Fifteen years ago, Kathleen wrote a poem to celebrate your wedding. Today, she will read a new poem:

Kathleen reads.

GERRY:

Sandy and PJ, I am going to repeat for you the vows you took 15 years ago and ask you to affirm them.

Of all the men and women you know, you have chosen each other as life partners. Knowing what you know of each other and trusting in what you do not yet know, are you ready to go forward in marriage?

SANDY AND PJ:

We are.

To guests

It is appropriate that you, the family and friends, are here to participate in this wedding. The ideals, the understanding, and the mutual respect which these two bring to this marriage have roots in the love, friendship, and guidance which you have provided them. Do you intend to continue with this support, please answer, "We do."

Response: We do.

Jim, will you make a toast and a blessing using the sweet cookie we each have taken.

Jim says words.
Please eat your cookies while we listen to a selection played by Maria and Paul.

PJ, please repeat after me.

Sandy, I want to live with you just as you are. I choose you above all others to share my life with me. I want to love you for yourself in the hope that you will become all that you can be. I promise to honor this pledge as long as life and faith endure.

Sandy, please repeat after me:

PJ, I want to live with you just as you are. I choose you above all others to share my life with me. I want to love you for yourself in the hope that you will become all that you can be. I promise to honor this pledge as long as life and faith endure.

As a symbol of your connection each to the other, I ask you to exchange rings.

Rings are an ancient symbol, round like the sun, like the eye, like the arms that embrace, an eternal circle — for love that is given comes back round again and again. Therefore, may these rings that you give to each other remind you that your love, like the sun, illuminates all that come near you in life; that your love, like the eye, must see clearly the path which you walk together; and that your love, like the arms with which you embrace and comfort, is a blessing upon this world.

Sandy, please repeat after me as you place this ring on PJ's finger:
This ring is a symbol that you are my beloved and you are my friend.

PJ, please repeat after me as you place this ring on Sandy's finger.
This ring is a symbol that you are my beloved and you are my friend.

With these rings you have recommitted yourself to the vows you took 15 years ago. May all honor your words and your choice of each other from the many men and women of this earth. Jose Marti wrote:

Love is born
with the pleasure of looking at each other,
it is fed
with the necessity
of seeing each other,
it is concluded with the impossibility
of ever being apart.

"Go hand in hand along the path you choose to walk together. Maintain a closeness to nature, a degree of simplicity, an awareness of beauty, and love for each other that will always permit you to look into each other's eyes and say that you would do it again."

Musicians play "We've Only Just Begun"

May you have long life and love and all the happiness that heaven can bring. Ladies and gentlemen, please join me in congratulating Sandy and PJ on the marriage they have built and on the future of their lives together.

Cheers and applause

Sandy and PJ, you may kiss.

There will be a receiving line at the pavilion. Sandy and PJ will lead us to the party.

Music plays and Sandy and PJ lead us to the party.

If it weren't true, it could be a story!

The story goes that in times of trouble, a great holy man would go to a sacred place in the forest, build a fire and say a prayer, and the world would be restored. When the holy man died, his disciples continued the tradition. They were not sure where to find the sacred site in the forest, but they built a fire and said the prayer. It was enough. When they died, no one knew the method to make the holy fire, but still the prayer was said, and it was enough. At last, even the prayer was forgotten, but the story remained. It was enough.

A ceremony is a form of storytelling. If you tell the story, it is enough.

Of course, not everyone has a talent for words. Not everyone has the good fortune to experience the events of an extraordinary and happy life. Chei and David have both talent and luck. When they contacted me to officiate at their recommitment ceremony, they wanted to acknowledge the thrill of their own journey together, and to celebrate the children and friends who had contributed so much to their shared life. Their wedding 32 years before had been a simple ceremony witnessed by David's parents, followed by Chinese food and an evening at their favorite piano bar in Greenwich Village. This time around they wanted to celebrate with panache. Flowers, food, wine, and music made an elegant party; but the real magic of the evening came from telling their unique love story. We rarely give ourselves a time to say what we feel, and when we try, we frequently become overwhelmed. We tend to describe our emotions. The story is enough.

As Chei and David talked with me, I realized I only needed to frame their story with the structure of ritual to give them and their family the chance to speak. The story would convey and highlight the emotions of the occasion. Stories do not have to be told in linear form. Image layered upon image will create an emotional narrative. Chei and David had always been great fans of the American song book. These classic lyrics are a part of our cultural resonance. We decided to have a piano tune echo me as I opened the ceremony with lyrics from Cole Porter, Marvin Hamlisch and Marilyn and Alan Bergman. These songs served as souvenirs of David and Chei's life together, triggering memories of places, occasions, and feelings they had shared together and with their family and friends who had witnessed their marriage over years. I am not a singer. The pianist echoed my words with the melody. I didn't hit the notes, but it was enough to speak the words as I shared the images that all the guests understood were the story of David and Chei's marriage.

In ancient times, the storytellers, priests and shamans were said to sing their songs. I am sure this was not the Belle Canto singing that we associate with entertainers today. Rather, I believe, it was the combining of image and rhythm into a repeated pattern, the creation of ceremony. Most officiants perform a ceremony with this sense of "speak singing." A clumsy speaker imposes an artificial pattern which levels the literal and emotional meaning of the words — (thus, the sing-song cadence that so often lulls us to sleep at speeches and religious services.) A good speaker, like a good singer, has a natural voice which captures the words and tells the story, which, if it is written by master lyricists, is well told. Everyone likes to listen to a well-told story no matter how well they already know it. I couldn't have asked for better lyricists or a better story.

Cole Porter's songs express this couple's exuberant affection. Every day, they say these words to each other, literally and figuratively. These lyrics express David and Chei's daily "I do." These are the songs in their hearts, the romantic impulse that energizes them to retell their story and remake their vows.

"Ordinary Miracles" is Chei's life story. She came to the U.S. from the poverty of Mexico, but her decency and kindness shone out, attracting a fairy godmother and a prince. If it weren't true, it could be a modern variant of the classic fairy tale. Cinderella is a story about appreciation and transformation. We are filled with Disney images of mice and pumpkins, but the real story is one of ashes, the cinders of loss and hardship, and the life force which moves us to pick ourselves up, clean ourselves, and go out to the dance of life. Everyone admires those who dance well. When the prince comes looking for his partner, he recognizes her because the shoe fits: not because she pushes herself forward, not because she looks like a princess, but because that symbol of the dance, the glass slipper that seems like it should be so fragile, reveals the extraordinary person who has the courage to wear it. The magic only happens because there is a pair. The prince must bring the lost slipper to Cinderella to restore her to her true self. His efforts are the catalyst for the magic to happen. So it was with David and Chei. So it is with a marriage. No one does it alone.

David and Chei wanted a recommitment ceremony to tell their story, to give voice to the happily ever after. Their ceremony offered a glimpse of the rich possibilities in their future life together and reminded everyone how impossible dreams can sometimes come true. How a mysterious fate can bring two people across the earth to meet and fall in love. The ceremony only needed to frame the statements which their children, their guests, and their life stories presented to evoke the magic of their love and to inspire all present to believe and love more.

Their daughter Kena says, "Ever since I was little I knew that there was something very special about your marriage — you could see it in the way that you looked at each other, or held hands walking down the street, in the way that you did everything together." Their son Jesse says, "Through the ups and downs in life, my parents' love for one another has been so great that it has overcome all obstacles. Love is such a strong emotion and difficult to put into words. My parents, standing here before you tonight, are a model of what love really should be, could be, and is."

David sent an invitation to his guests three months before the party. He said, "Thirty-two years later, I thought I'd try it again…On Sept 4th, I will once again propose, and yes …this time I'll bring a ring with me! Optimistic that Chei's answer will be "yes," I've planned a hopefully more intimate and appropriate affair for our second time around — a romantic candlelight dinner with our family and a few friends, including Gershwin,

Porter, Arlen, Billy, and Ella. As this is truly a surprise until I propose, I ask your help in keeping the secret."

Ritual speaks to eternal truths. Like the physical truth of our expansive universe of stars and planets, love expands to include all in its circle. Just as their life together had expanded to include other bodies, David included his children and friends in this ceremony from beginning to end, from big bang to the unknown. Following the pattern of this story, the ceremony actually begins with this invitation, the shared secret, and everyone's anticipation of the proposal. It evolves three months later into the witnessed vows and the promise of continued expansion into whatever the time and the universe will bring.

Chei says to David, "Please accept my love, my devotion, my soul forever and ever… past ever."

David says to Chei, "You are, without question, the great love of my life, and I will love and cherish you always. There is simply nothing within my power I wouldn't do for you."

And I say, "Please repeat after me the words that were, that are, that always will be true."

The only words left to say as everyone joins this couple for a drink will be the Jewish toast L'chaim — To Life!

RECOMMITMENT CEREMONY FOR CHEI (MARIA GUADALUPE VIAMAR GARCIA DE FR.) AND DAVID FR. DECEMBER 4, 2004 LOMBARDY HOTEL, NEW YORK CITY

Guests are ushered into their seats.

GERRY:

Good evening, I am Gerald Fierst, Civil Celebrant. Tonight, on behalf of our hosts David and Chei, I invite all of you to fall in love. Lyricists forever attempt to describe love. Cole Porter wrote:

Birds do it. Bees do it.
Even educated fleas do it.
Let's do it. Let's fall in love.

He also wrote:

You're the top!
You're the Coliseum,.
You're the top!
You're the Louvre Museum.
You're a melody from a symphony by Strauss.
You're a Bendel bonnet,
A Shakespeare sonnet,
You're Mickey Mouse.

But there's a more obscure lyric from Marvin Hamlisch and Marilyn and Alan Bergman which David and Chei feel speaks to their love:

Change can come on tiptoe,
Love is where it starts.
It resides, often hides
deep within our hearts.

Ordinary Miracles
happen all around.
Just by giving and receiving
comes belonging and believing

Hope can spring eternally,
plant it and it grows,
Love is all that's necessary,
Love in it's extraordinary way,
Makes ordinary miracles
every bless-ed day.

(Begin "Body and Soul")

Let us join together tonight to celebrate the miracle of Chei and David's love.

(The French doors are opened by the three children, Daniel, Olivia, and Karla, who hand Chei flowers and place a boutonniere on David. David and Chei walk down the aisle to Gerry. Kena and Jesse help the children to their parents and then join the party on either side of Gerry.)

GERRY:

Chei, you have many names — your friends and family here in the east call you
Chei. In Mexico, you are Maria Guadalupe. And on the west coast, you are Lupita.
David, you are David. But together, you stand here tonight simply as man and wife.
Thirty-four years ago, Suzanna Gabagda, a reader of palms, of horoscopes and of
the tarot, gave Chei the card of an American woman Josephine Lees. After a harsh
journey, Chei came to New York City penniless and friendless. She remembered
that card and found that woman. Josephine saw Chei and opened her heart as a
mother would greet a daughter; and Chei looked at Josephine's great soul and loved
her immediately as a daughter would a mother. Josephine welcomed Chei into her
home without reservation. She immediately contacted her network of friends who
donated and helped to buy anything Chei needed. Then, Josephine helped Chei
locate a job as a governess and sponsored her so that she could stay in the U.S.,
get an education, and learn English at the International House in New York City.

Meantime, David, who was working on the design for the U.S. pavilion at the
World's Fair in Osaka, had come to the center to pick up some Japanese. David
spoke no Spanish. Chei spoke no Japanese and little English, but fate and love
intervened and brought them together one evening. What was the language of
love? David drew, and Chei said "Uh huh."

The evening lingered into night until, at last, David had to take Chei to the bus stop,
and as they said goodbye, David, you say you knew at that moment that this was
the woman with whom you wanted to spend the rest of your life. And Chei, you say
that you knew at that moment that this was the man you had seen years before in a
dream. You recognized in David the kindness, the creativity, the caring, that was the
fulfillment of that dream.

David, in 1972, you were on photo assignment in Ireland. You sent Chei a postcard
that read, "I miss you. I love you."

Upon your return, you found that Chei had similar ideas. In that one week, while
you were away, your kitchen had been repainted and your closets had somehow
become Chei's. Ever since — over a marriage of 32 years — you have remained
inseparable. You, David and Chei, have produced two terrific children, Kena and
Jesse, who stand here with you tonight. Together, you have faced both the challenges
and enjoyed the rewards that life brings to us all.

The great Cuban poet Jose Marti wrote:
Love is born with the pleasure of looking at each other.
It is fed with the necessity of seeing each other.
It is concluded with the impossibility of ever being apart.

Chei and David, your children wish to toast your love and offer their own words and perspective on your marriage.

(The children each take a flute of champagne that has been waiting on a small table and give one to each parent and keep one for themselves.)

KENA:

First I'd like to say how lucky, and honored Jesse and I are to have you as our parents. We look at the relationship that the two of you have and see something that is very special and very rare. The two of you have always been inseparable — we see that you are partners in life in the truest sense, and your devotion to one another has been an extraordinary example for both of us. Your love for one another has extended to me and Jesse, and we are surrounded by your love and dedication to this family.

Ever since I was little I knew that there was something very special about your marriage — you could see it in the way that you looked at each other, or held hands walking down the street, in the way that you did everything together. And when you'd talk about one another, you'd do it with such pride and admiration that it could only come from the true happiness you've found together. I look at your marriage and see that you have shared what everyone aspires to have in their own — unequivocal love, respect, devotion, and happiness.

JESSE:

Family and Friends:

Hello, I'm their son, Jesse.

As you probably all know, my dad is in advertising and has been, for at least as long as I can remember. I learned from him that the best way to ensure you get a message across is to repeat it.

It seems that my mother and father are trying to tell us something, again.

Guys, we get it. You really love each other.

I also learned that it is very important to clearly define your target audience and get your message so they will see it.

Thirty-two years ago, the only people who they truly valued to share their message of love with them were the four or five guests they had at their wedding.

Today, however, there are so many more friends and family with whom they would like to share that same message.

All of you seated before me now, have in some way enriched the lives of my parents since the first time they exchanged vows.

So in a way, today is also a day that my parents can honor the vows of friendship they made with so many of you over the past 32 years.

I know they feel honored that each of you can be here with them today.

So what makes today so much more of a special day than the first time around?

The fact is, when my mother and father met, they were just two individuals.

But by being there for each other over the years, they have helped each other grow into the wonderful people they are today.

They entered into this relationship with hopes, wishes and dreams.

They probably had a wonderful life living these dreams, before my sister and I showed up. Since then, it's been nothing but anxiety, ulcers, tension headaches, panic attacks, bad backs, hernias, hair loss, and many sleepless nights we kept them up past our curfew.

If there is one thing I learned from my parents, it is how to get on their last nerve and live to tell about it.

But most importantly, from both, my mother and my father, I have learned, watched, and appreciated the importance of having love in your life.

Through the ups and downs in life, my parents' love for one another has been so great that it has overcome all obstacles. Love is such a strong emotion and difficult to put into words. My parents, standing here before you tonight, are a model of what love really should be, could be, and is.

So in the words of Frank Sinatra:

"The greatest thing you'll ever learn, is just to love, and be loved, in return."

Thank You.

GERRY:

Your actual wedding was lunch at David's parents, an evening in the Village, Dim-Sum in Chinatown, then, back to work the next day. Tonight, the setting has changed, but the feelings are the same, and even stronger, even more heartfelt, true, and precious today than they were then.

David and Chei, I know you each have something to say to each other.

CHEI:

My dearest sweet darling,

For more than 20 years, life was making sure that I would end up no farther than any of the thousands of people around me. It was kind of a dark time in my life, but I also had a father who, even though he was an alcoholic, always believed in me and gave me so much love and words that gave me a lot of confidence. He would continually say that if I really wanted something out of life I would get it, and that I should work hard to get it because almost everything was reachable. And so being always a big dreamer I had many dreams to keep me going, just that he did not know exactly what my dream was. It was kind of silly to want something that was only a fairy tale. I read Cinderella and that's what I wanted: I wanted a beautiful prince, smart, gentle and that would love me very much.

I left Mexico, not knowing that at that moment a true fairy tale was about to begin. I arrived with a series of problems, very little money, no friends, no clothes. No, absolutely nothing. Then magic happened! My fairy godmother appeared, and swished all over New York with her magic wand, and everything came at once. For the first time in my life, I had a feeling of having a real mom, loving and supportive. Her name is Josephine. I had clothes, a home with a warm bed, and even an alarm clock that would awake me with music; better teachers at school, a job, and an invitation to join the International Center, which I'll call the castle where a meeting was about to happen with my fairy-tale prince.

And so finally the day came for the ball and… There he was, so tall, so beautiful, gorgeous eyes, great voice, great everything! I was simply swept away by his presence, things just seemed to disappear around us, and it was just my prince and myself. And just a few months later, he married me and, the story did not end there. It was just about to begin. He has always been there for me when I need a Husband, a Lover, a Friend and just about the best companion for travel or just taking a simple walk. He has been giving me so much love and happiness. He gave me just about anything that my imagination would come up with. He also gave me the most precious gifts of all: two shiny beautiful stars, and we named them Kena and Jesse, who have made our life even more beautiful.

I thank God, for this wonderful life of mine, and ask him to help me to make happy my wonderful husband. I know I cannot re-pay all his love and great things that he has done for me. So today in front of our children, the best MOM in the world, and this group of family and friends, I want you to know that I adore you and that I appreciate and treasure everything you have done for me, and the troubles you have gone thru to make me the happiest of all living creatures.

PLEASE ACCEPT MY LOVE, MY DEVOTION AND MY SOUL FOREVER AND EVER….past ever…

Your Chei

DAVID:

Tonight we celebrate a lifetime together,
and a lifetime of memories fill my mind.

Milestone Memories:
The births of our children.
Listening together to Billie Holiday throughout your labor with Kena.
Jesse's extraordinarily sudden entry into the world
as a physician rushed into the delivery room just in the nick of time
to catch him with one hand, as he shot forth.
Your first introduction to snow at age 25, and how very excited you
were in throwing snowballs at me
Jesse's first car. Kena's graduation.

Tender Memories:
That warm, wonderful, indelible smile you wear so very well
Your gentle touch
Our countless and unforgettable strolls through Central Park
Sitting on our favorite stoop on East 79th street
eating cantaloupe ice cream with the kids
Romantic dinners out, cozy movies in
Holding hands

Dear, wonderful Josephine Memories:
Those brisk walks with her on Coast Boulevard
Her delight in serving us Bon Bons at the end of every meal
Her two nightly scotches: two fingers of scotch, one finger of water,
a little ice.
Our trip together through Spain.
Listening mesmerized to tales of her exotic travels
to the ends of the earth
Our introduction to the Kirns, our wonderful West Coast family
Those amazing carefree summers with her and Helen and Betty
in Rhode Island

Simply every single, solitary moment with this truly amazing woman

Only-in-New-York Memories:
The time Dustin Hoffman tried to pick you up
and you were so angry that I hadn't punched him in the nose.
The morning you left me eating breakfast alone
to go sit and have a long chat with Robert Redford
Your discussion with Paul Simon about natural childbirth...
all the time thinking that he worked in my office.
Conversations with Alberta Hunter between her sets at the Cookery
Bobby Short at the Carlyle.
Those countless evenings listening to Howard tickle the ivories
at the Surf Maid

Only-Chei-Would-Do-That memories
The afternoon you served a full-course dinner for the four of us
complete with two lit candelabras, on the rocks of a Woodstock creek

Funny Memories:
The time in Istanbul we decided to have a Turkish bath and mistakenly
walked into a high school to ask for one

Even Embarrassing Memories:
The evening we spent hours at the Andersons waiting for a dinner we
hadn't been invited to. Poor Bob thinking perhaps his wife had neglected
to tell him we were coming, and too embarrassed to ask why we were there.

Sad Memories:
The death of my father.
The passing of yours, as well as your mother's just months ago

Exotic Memories:
Traveling the world together...from Buenos Aries to Dubrovnik,
Prague to Monte Carlo, Lisbon to Vienna, Athens to Granada,
Uruguay to Paris, Madrid to St Lucia...
and just about everywhere in between.
Memorable evenings
That magical dinner atop the Eden Hotel overlooking Rome
New Year's in San Marco's where we poured Champagne for everyone
in glasses we had brought especially for the occasion
Our three-hour Christmas Eve dinner at Toutoune in Paris with the kids,
and the long wonderful walk back to our hotel
at two in the morning through the quiet wet Parisian streets
That magical evening in Madrid eating under the moonlight
And of course, every evening we've ever spent in Venice and Rome,
and on and on...
These memories and a multitude more are simply irreplaceable to me

More than three decades of living, working and traveling with you have only
confirmed what I've always known.

That is, that a childhood far, far less than ideal, has armed you with an
uncommon and unbreakable inner strength and the ability to survive most of life's
hurdles with grace, optimism, practicality and above all...almost always a smile.

Those of us who know of your journey from Mexico may have mistakenly
concluded that you arrived at our shore with very little:

It's an easy mistake to make. Just look at the facts.

No family waited for you with open arms
No network of friends was here to support you
You arrived with little formal education, no immediate job possibilities,
unable to speak our language and...very little money.
You carried only a small suitcase of summer clothes
to protect you from the harsh New York winter

But I've come to realize that IF that was what we thought,
our beliefs were terribly misguided.

Because the truth is, young lady,
you arrived here with far, far more than most
and just about everything you would need to succeed.

You came armed with more hope and optimism than I have ever
seen in one human being
with the unstoppable energy of a dozen
inherent kindness an endlessly positive attitude towards living
the deepest desire to learn about absolutely everything
the guts to work hard...very, very hard to build that better life
an innate sense of style
and the unbreakable pride your father Cliserio instilled in you —
look down on no one, but up to none

But most importantly, you arrived here...and to me
with the world's brightest brown eyes,
the most beautiful smile
and the biggest and warmest heart

All of us here tonight have each come a long way in our own lives.
But fate, as it does, asks some to travel farther than others.
And I suspect that few, if any of us here, have traveled the distance
you have, from where you started to where you've come.
Beside us stand our two children.
We revel in their accomplishments
and the way they continue to conduct their lives.
We look forward to their continued happiness and success.
To Kena's upcoming marriage to Joe, Jesse's new career
and all the great and wonderful things life will hopefully bring
them both

and...maybe even a few grandchildren for us

You are, without question, the great love of my life
and I will love and cherish you always.

There is simply nothing within my power I wouldn't do for you.

I'm a very, very, very lucky man indeed.

GERRY:

David, please repeat after me the words that were, that are, that always will be true.

(*David repeats*)

I, David, take you, Chei,
to be my wife,
to have and to hold,
from this day forward,
for better or worse,
for richer or poorer,
in sickness and in health,
for the rest of my life.
Chei, I give you my eternal love and my eternal devotion. I give you my heart.

GERRY:

Chei, please repeat after me the words that were, that are, that will always be true.

(*Chei repeats*)

I, Chei, take you, David,
to be my husband,
to have and to hold,
from this day forward,
for better or worse,
for richer or poorer,
in sickness and in health,
for the rest of my life.
David, I give you my eternal love and my eternal devotion. I give you my heart.

GERRY:

Rings are an ancient symbol, round like the sun, like the eye, like the arms that embrace, an eternal circle — for love that is given comes back round again and again. David and Chei, when you were married 32 years ago, your wedding rings were second hand, but their simplicity didn't diminish their meaning. These rings have symbolized and accompanied your love, which like the sun, illuminates all that come near you in life; which like the eye sees clearly the path which you walk together; which like your arms, embrace and comfort. May your love be golden and never tarnish. May you hand in hand, dance with the music of life, and, as you travel to the ends of the world, may you always come full circle to the home which is together with each other.

Kena and Jesse, please give your parents their rings.

David, please take this ring which Chei has worn for 32 years and repeat after me as you replace it upon her finger:

My life and love are bound forever to you.

DAVID:

My life and love are bound forever to you.

GERRY:

Chei, please take this ring which David has worn for 32 years and repeat after me as you replace it upon his finger:

My life and love are bound forever to you.

CHEI:

My life and love are bound forever to you.

GERRY:

Ladies and gentlemen, please join me in congratulating David and Chei on the marriage they have built and on the future of their lives together.

(Audience applauds. Music begins "Fascinating Rhythm." David and Chei exit)

Please join David and Chei in the bar for a drink.

Narrative and metaphor are the foundation of ritual, triggering the hopes and dreams and fears we hold deep within the psyche. A ceremony of recommitment and renewal should fill us with the symbolic facts of two shared lives, telling an accumulation story culminating with a restatement of vows; but a restatement *isn't* just a summing up. It is a reevaluation of the substance that has given worth to a marriage, showing the profits and losses as they truly exist, and the potential which lies in the future. Through story, symbol, and metaphor, we celebrate the past, and affirm the now, the threshold moment to which we have come; and, by looking to the past, we understand the choice to step into the future. By symbolically sharing the complexities of a life's story within our whole circle of friends and family, we summon the strength of love to take us into the unknown, confident that, come what may, a shared love will be the value which will preserve and sustain.

As the poet says, "I love thee with the breath, smiles, tears, of all my life! — and, if God choose, I shall but love thee better after death."

Chapter Eight

WHAT IS
A MARRIAGE?

I recently performed a wedding at a hospice in New York City. The bride and groom had two children and had lived together for seven years. His liver was failing, and no one was sure if he would live out the day. A special license was issued by a judge, and the wedding took place 15 minutes after it was valid. Family and friends gathered around as I read the required monitum:

Before you are legally joined together in my presence and in the presence of these, your family and friends, I am bound to remind you publicly of the solemn, the serious, and the binding nature of the relationship into which you are now about to enter. It is made in the deepest sense to the exclusion of all others, and it is entered into with the desire, the hope, and the firm intention that it will last for life.

No one could hold back the tears, but after the vows, the groom's mother said the traditional Jewish wish, "Mazel Tov." Good luck! Congratulations!

I have thought about this wedding a great deal. What is marriage? The groom had hours to live. By marrying, he gave his wife certain legal recourse for social services. Is that why they married? If so, why did the bride wear a special dress? The groom wore a tuxedo shirt. The families had bottles of sparkling grape juice to pop open after the ceremony. One of the rewards of being a civil celebrant is that you get to see the truth of humanity, which is not self-serving, but reaches out to connect. We desire the greater sense of self that comes from family, friends and community. This couple was not making a business decision to marry. They were reaching out for eternity.

The Ideal

What is a marriage? The conservative Heritage Foundation defines marriage by its benefits: "stability and meaning to human relationships," "the ideal for raising children," "transferring culture and civilization into future generations," and "a social institution of great public concern." I do not believe that marriage should be defined by its social product. The subtext here is that marriage is a legally sanctioned relationship between one man and one woman that defines our function within society. Political and religious conservatives may advance this definition to justify their personal and political agendas; they wish to impose on our philosophically and culturally diverse nation a legal framework for marriage which matches the traditional Christian pattern; but traditional long-term heterosexual households are no longer the status quo of our families. Cohabitation, divorce, and single-parenting have redefined our communities and our acceptance of the relationships that create a household, a good neighbor, and a good parent.

Ultimately, the decision to be a couple and to marry is a personal decision that cannot be defined by government or religious authorities, but comes from the need to recognize the special connection between two people when they choose to attach their individual identities to make a third identity: i.e. We are a couple. In doing so, they are not primarily saying we will pay taxes together or even have children together. Rather, they are saying we will have a life that incorporates your identity with mine. For whatever time they had together as husband and wife, my hospice couple forever and fundamentally changed who they were.

Faith

I do not subscribe to the liturgy of any religion when I acknowledge my belief that there is an energy which we call faith and soul. Marriage is an act of faith. We identify ourselves as a couple because we feel that our souls will be transformed and enlarged by being together with another person, rather than being alone. We have no proof for our belief; we have no guarantee. We act upon faith, a belief that is not grounded in rational consideration, but is based upon the energy we feel when we are intimate with the other person: That faith activates us to be together and expands our sense of being, our soul.

When my hospice couple married, even though their physical connection was temporal, their souls were changed. When we wished them mazel tov, we weren't wishing them future money and comfort. We were acknowledging the good fortune that had given their souls the opportunity to be together even for a brief moment. We were recognizing the fortune that had allowed their transformation into a couple and enriched their souls. The physical world is ever changing and impermanent, but that moment of union was a blessing beyond the measure of time.

Dissolution and Transformation

So, are we lessened when we fall out of love? When marriages dissolve and we change again? I believe that each moment describes who we are. It gives us the opportunity to decide if that is what we want to be. Our souls are transformative, and change reapportions the moments of our lives. We are not the same soul today as tomorrow, and we will not be the same soul in 20 years that we are today. I do not think divorce is casual, but I do not think the dissolution of a marriage negates the faith that made us act and fulfilled our souls. Even when trauma and heartbreak occur, somehow faith can linger in our hearts. Somehow faith reasserts itself and encourages us to seek fulfillment of our souls once again. The energy of choice is expansive, taking us into the future, without leaving the past behind. The wish is that fulfillment of the soul will always be a part of the relationship that makes us a couple. But such is not always the case, and, then, we must retain the positive faith that moves us into the future while leaving the negative energy of disappointment and mistrust behind. As much as we mark the beginning, we also must mark the ending of a relationship. In doing so, we acknowledge the energy that has defined our sense of soul and is now a part of who we are. In fact, I am sometimes asked to perform a divorce ceremony, not denying the past, but encouraging the energy which now carries into the future.

The Big Bang

In the preceding paragraphs, I have offered a metaphysical explanation of the love that leads to marriage; I have come to these thoughts by listening to couple after couple tell me their story. As I hear the history of these couples, I recognize the patterns of the great stories of world folklore and their connection to the physical world in which we live. The great myths are not that different from physical science. Expansion is the law of the universe, starting with the big bang and reaching out into the infinite. So our consciousness reaches far beyond us and even beyond memory.

The great Bengali Nobel laureate Rabindranath Tagore lyrically wrote:

Unending Love
I seem to have loved you in numberless forms, numberless times...
In life after life, in age after age, forever.
My spellbound heart has made and remade the necklace of songs,
That you take as a gift, wear round your neck in your many forms,
In life after life, in age after age, forever.

Whenever I hear old chronicles of love, it's age old pain,
It's ancient tale of being apart or together.
As I stare on and on into the past, in the end you emerge,
Clad in the light of a pole-star, piercing the darkness of time.
You become an image of what is remembered forever.

You and I have floated here on the stream that springs from the fount.
At the heart of time, love of one for another.
We have played along side millions of lovers,
Shared in the same shy sweetness of meeting,
the distressful tears of farewell,
Old love but in shapes that renew and renew forever.

The Story Goes

Poets, priests, magicians, and physicists use different terms, but find parallel images of time, space, and consciousness. While each life is unique, the pattern is repeated over and over again. The old story goes:

Once there was a beautiful queen named Silver Tree who had a daughter named Gold Tree who was even more beautiful. One day as they walked together in the garden by a fresh stream, a trout came to the surface of the water and said, 'Queen you are beautiful, but your daughter is the most beautiful one of all."

Life is an act of creation. As we pass through its garden, we may be surprised that we are not always the most special one of all. Sometimes we rejoice at the news, for we can become more by the gifts that a companion or child brings; and sometimes we are consumed by jealousy and regret.

Silver Tree was consumed by jealousy. She went to her husband the King and said, "Give me the heart and liver of Gold Tree."

The King quickly arranged a marriage for Gold Tree to a powerful prince who lived in a far-off land. He sent the girl off secretly and then presented Silver Tree with the heart and liver of a deer. Silver Tree was content that she was now the most beautiful one of all.

When energy is not expansive, it becomes self-deluded and destructive, consuming the life and soul around it.

A year passed, Silver Tree was walking in the garden, and the trout came to the surface of the stream. "Am I not beautiful?" Silver Tree asked. "You are, but Gold Tree is more beautiful," said the trout. "Gold Tree is dead. I have eaten her heart and liver," laughed Silver Tree. "No," the trout replied. "She lives in a far-off land and is married to a powerful prince."

One cannot deny truth.

Silver Tree quickly outfitted a ship and sailed it herself to the far-off land where Gold Tree was now happily married. When Gold Tree saw the sails on the horizon, she grew frightened and locked herself in her room. Silver Tree landed and came looking for her. "Will my own daughter deny me and not even let me give her a kiss in greeting?" she cried through the key hole. Gold Tree stuck her pinky finger through the key hole so that Silver Tree might kiss it. When she did so, Silver tree stuck a poisoned thorn under her daughter's finger nail, and Gold Tree fell down as if dead. Silver Tree then sailed back home; she was content.

All the characters in a story are ourselves. Sometimes we would kill that which is most beautiful in our lives, deceiving ourselves that destruction is better than transformation and expansion.

When the prince found Gold Tree lying on the floor, he mourned her deeply. He could not bear to bury her, but laid her on the bed, and kept her in that locked room where he would come every night to look upon her face.

The past does not disappear.

Eventually, the prince remarried.

But life moves on.

The new wife sensed that her husband was troubled, but did not understand his sadness until one day he left the door to Gold Tree's room unlocked. Curious, she entered the room and found Gold Tree lying there in a death-like sleep. Only a thorn sticking under the sleeping princess's little fingernail marred her perfect beauty. The new wife pulled the thorn out, and, suddenly, Gold Tree awoke.

True soul recognizes the totality of experience and acts to restore, not deny.

Gold Tree told her story. The Prince was overjoyed to see her restored, but when the new wife prepared to leave, he stopped her and insisted that they all live together, which they did quite happily.

Truth acknowledged is the first step to renewal.

Meantime, Silver Tree was walking in the garden when the trout surfaced to say, "Gold Tree is more beautiful than you." "You don't know of what you speak. Gold Tree is no more," answered the Queen. "She is awake and happy," answered the trout. Immediately, Silver Tree set sail to the far distant shore where Gold Tree lived. When Gold Tree saw the sails on the horizon, she recognized her mother's approach and grew frightened, but the new wife said, "Fear not, follow me. I will keep you safe."

Eventually, renewal will demand transformation and growth. We must face that which threatens us.

When Silver Tree's ship docked, the new wife took Gold Tree down to the dock to greet its arrival. "Daughter," the Queen said as she came down the gangplank, "Here is a cup of wine I have prepared for us to share so that we may salute your good health." The Queen offered Gold Tree a goblet of poisoned wine, but the new wife stepped forward. "In this land, the guest drinks first," and she lifted the cup up to the Queen's mouth. Immediately, the wine touched the Queen's lips, and she fell dead upon the dock.

Gold Tree and the new wife are, in truth, symbols of the same soul at different stages of awareness. The vulnerability of Gold Tree is the soul who marries without consciousness of the pressures life will bring. Her only defense is to hide. The new wife understands that love will only survive when it meets threatening danger and stands strong.

Gold Tree, the second wife, and the Prince lived happily from that day forth, pleased and peaceful.

These three characters represent the parts of one integrated soul. The reality of marriage is more complicated than courtship. Marriage survives because of truth in the face of adversity and acceptance of the unexpected. The whole of life's experiemces are housed in a marriage.

Politics and Soul

In the current national debate on the state of marriage in the U.S., social conservatives argue that a national tolerance for diverse lifestyles and the diminished influence of traditional religious values have contributed to the statistical decrease in married, two-parent households. Marriage, they argue, is the cornerstone of society — by which they mean traditional heterosexual married couples are the best for the raising of children. Therefore, they justify restricting the emotional, social and legal benefits of marriage in the hope of controlling social behavior through denial to others of the very rights they enjoy. An evolving world is not the enemy of marriage. The human spirit aspires to build and go on into the future. If the soul is nurtured, the family will grow, and the whole community will be enriched.

I am not a sociologist. I cannot argue about the effectiveness of social engineering; but, as a celebrant, I do understand the power of ritual to give meaning and direction to one's life. I have observed that when people marry, they take their words seriously. The soul awareness of Gold Tree and the second wife is to go out and take responsibility to face the truth; having done so their lives are awake and aware. Marriage creates a sense of awareness beyond self. The public act of voicing commitment and connection changes the way one sees the world and begins the task of taking responsibility as a couple to make a life together. Whether celebrated with a traditional religious ceremony or with a meaningful civil ceremony, I believe giving a couple the opportunity to marry makes for a more stable civil society.

A meaningful wedding ceremony marks the life passage of marriage as the beginning of a transformative journey where one assumes new life responsibility. Some will succeed, and some will fail. Some will be wiser, kinder, gentler, than others, and these couples will be of all kinds. Not everyone makes a fit parent; not every marriage will survive; but everyone deserves the chance to experience their humanity by connecting their humanity to another with the blessing of friends, family, and community. Ultimately, our national crises of child welfare and education do not stem from the diversity of couples who desire to marry, or the diversity of lifestyles in and out of marriage, but rather from the cultural priorities upon which our political leadership chooses to act. What real political action results from our debate about marriage as a building block of society and the foundation for child welfare? The words are mouthed, but education and child-health expenditures are short changed; child care and social services are curtailed. The increasing prevalence of divorced and single-parent households does not come from diverse life choices, but from hard economic and social truths. It is for good reason that the divorce rate is less in households with more income and education.

The Buddha Said

Prince Siddhartha said there is no enlightenment without endowment. I believe being able to marry is a fundamental right. Marriage endows our souls so that our lives are enriched and expanded by the experience of our humanity. Each of us deserves the right to endow our souls with the treasure of a life partner. I cannot define a marriage by its form; what makes a marriage is its being — its soul. Thus, I deplore the Federal law known as the Defense of Marriage Act by which the Congress has defined marriage exclusively between a man and a woman, and authorized any state to deny the validity of a same-sex union which has been authorized by another state. Equally, I deplore the cowardice of state legislatures who will authorize civil unions, but fear the use of the word "marriage," as if marriage takes only one form.

Look at a few of the many variations marriage does take in 21st Century America.

I have a friend who was married for 25 years. He lived in New York City and his wife lived in Paris. They never had children, but still found their **long-distance marriage** fulfilling and happy.

I have another friend who has never registered his marriage legally. Yet, he has lived in a **common-law** marriage with his wife for 30 years. They have no children of their own, but together they have raised her children from a previous marriage.

I know of a famous actress whose marriage of almost 40 years has included numerous affairs by both partners. They have agreed to this **polyamorous** life style even as they have raised children and maintained a successful household.

I know of several high-powered executive couples who are married but have chosen to be **childless**. Their priorities are their life as a couple and their individual professional careers. They have chosen to bypass the experience of parenthood.

I know both lesbian and gay couples who have accepted the legal limitations of **civil union** and created marriages which include raising children.

These are only the variations of marriage that I have observed first-hand. Within our society, there are numerous legal and illegal variations of married households.

Arkansas, Arizona, and Louisiana have created **covenant marriage** which restricts the ability to divorce. Of course, couples can simply cross into another state to dissolve these marriages.

Despite being against the law and discouraged by the religious establishment, **plural marriage or polygamy** is practiced by as many as 100,000 American Muslims and 30,000 to 40,000 renegade Mormon households.

Society's acceptance of the right to divorce makes **serial marriage** common. Almost everyone can speak of a celebrity, neighbor, co-worker, friend or family member who has been married two, three, or even four times, and looks forward to being married again.

A Good Beginning

When I list all the forms of marriage that I know exist in our society, I only do so to contradict the hypocrisy of the social critics who would narrowly define marriage to suit their personal agenda.

Most of my clients come to me envisioning a marriage in which they will grow together, make a life together, and be old together. Why would I refuse anyone who came to me with that vision? I firmly believe that the purpose of a wedding ceremony is to express the emotional truth of this choice. My clients come from all over the world and from a diversity of traditions, but whatever their backgrounds, they come seeking the power of words to express the importance of this moment in their lives. They sense that their desire to be together is part of an expansive energy and that the words of a ceremony actualize into a good beginning for their journey together. The rest is a mystery for life to reveal.

What is Marriage?

And so it is told:

Before the before, and before the beginning of time, in a valley of green hills and rich fields of grain, there was a man who lived a life of plenty without questions or worry. His cows were his pride — beautiful white cows with great horns, who gave him rich milk every day — but one day his cows went dry. And the next day the cows were dry. And the next day.

"Someone is stealing my milk," he thought. "I must catch the thief." And so he did not return home, but lay upon the ground and waited.

The sun set. The stars shone. The man fell asleep, only to be awakened by the sound of singing and laughing. Looking up into the sky, he saw a rope of starlight dropped from the heavens, with beautiful women descending to the earth. They ran to his cows, and began to milk.

"Stop thieves!" he shouted The women ran and began to climb back into the sky, but the man ran faster and caught the last one by her heel and pulled her back to earth.

"You have taken my milk. How will you pay me for what was not yours?"

The woman looked at the earth in shame. "You are right. I must repay you for what has been taken away. I will stay and work for you, keeping your house, cooking, and cleaning, and caring for you."

The man looked at the woman. She was fair. "Stay with me, then," he said.

So she stayed on the earth to serve the man. He would watch her do her tasks, listening to her singing as she moved with grace through the days and nights of work. Soon he fell in love with her.

"Woman, stay with me and marry me for you are fair, and good, and bring me much delight."

"Man," she replied, "I too am happy with you. I will stay here, if you will make one promise to me."

"Anything," he laughed.

"I have a box which I brought from the stars. It is all I have of my home in the skies. It is mine. You must never open it and look inside."

"Woman, woman, foolish woman, what a small thing you ask of me. Yes, yes, this promise is easy. What do I care what you keep inside that box? Why should I look inside to see what you keep there? It is yours, and so it will always be."

And so they became husband and wife and lived happily for many days.

But one day when the woman was away, the man began to think, "That box, that box, what can be hidden there? What secret is this woman keeping from me? How would she know if I took one look? "

And curiosity called the man to the corner where the woman kept her things. Taking the box in his hand, he opened its lid to look inside.

"NOTHING," he began to laugh and shout, "NOTHING," he looked and saw, "NOTHING. Foolish woman, silly woman, you have tried to trick me. There is nothing in the box, but you will never know that I looked."

So the man returned the box to its place and did not say a word when the woman returned at dark.

She entered the house and looked at his face and knew. "You have looked," she said, and turned back through the door.

"Wait, woman, wait, there was nothing there. Don't be angry. The joke is on me. I saw there was nothing."

A silver chord dropped from the sky. The woman began to climb.

"Wait, woman, wait. Why must you go? I looked, I am sorry, but the box was empty. Stay with me. Do not be angry because of nothing."

The woman stopped her climb and turned to the man. "Man, it is not that you looked; it is that you looked and could not see."

Then the woman climbed back into the sky, leaving the man alone upon the earth, and since that time human kind has looked at the stars, wandering and wondering what is there that we cannot see.

Chapter Nine

BLASTS —
THE BEST WEDDINGS

Nationally, the average wedding costs between $20,000 and $30,000. In metropolitan areas like New York, Los Angeles and Chicago, the cost ranges far higher. I remember attending a wedding on Long Island that I am sure cost close to $250,000. Lavish flower arrangements decorated the ceremony. Expensive bouquets were provided for the eight bridesmaids. The bridal gown alone probably ran more than $5,000. The party started with a cocktail reception and buffet that could have served as dinner. The elegant dinner that followed included choices of appetizer, main course, and dessert. A band and singers entertained with a dance leader and two dance assistants who relentlessly encouraged everyone to fill the dance floor. The noise was so loud guests couldn't converse at their tables. One was forced to join the party plan or be pounded by sound. Somewhere near dawn, a second set of tables was rolled into the party with more drinks, more desserts, and the option of omelets. At dawn, as we traveled home, we felt numbed by the conspicuous consumption. As we stopped at a traffic light, a beggar came over to our window and stood silently with his hand out. I reached into my wallet and pulled out a bill. How could I not give him something after what I had seen consumed that evening? Obviously, this is an extreme case of wedding mania. Obviously, taste and standards vary from person to person. Obviously, the choice is yours.

Simplicity and Imagination

I am not comfortable with spending in one night the equivalent of a new car (sometimes a very expensive new car) or the down payment on a home. Wedding parties have grown fatter and richer as America has experienced its past half century of prosperity. The wedding industry has connected weddings to extravagance and consumption. It has created a perception that the wedding party is appropriately one of the major purchases of a couple's life. Ultimately, I believe simplicity and imagination make a stronger state-ment than pretense. Having seen the preparations for hundreds of weddings, I have come to realize that the commercial wedding industry sells the conventional style of the big wedding party as the ultimate dream. It will encourage you to spend as much money as you can to capture this dream without really offering anything that reflects the romance, commitment, and individuality of the occasion. I go to dozens of weddings a year. I realize I am jaded, but carving boards, pasta stations, and chocolate fountains, no matter how tasty, are so redundant that I cynically wonder if they aren't left over from the last party. The wedding industry will tell you it offers the usual assortment of roasts, *and* fish, *and* chicken, *and* steak, to meet the popular taste, and to offer economies of scale. In truth, I suspect the cost is reflective of what the market will bear. My message is **Don't be afraid to think outside the box.**

I make this argument knowing that many mothers will say, "I *want* this for my daughter." Many daughters will gladly concur in the romantic vision of the white wedding. I make this argument not to discourage the party, but to encourage consider-ation of the party as a continuation of the ceremony's celebration. The point of it all is to share the moment. Your guests are there because they love you. They will fill the simplest celebration with joy.

Make yourself available to enjoy the day. If you can, hire an executive assistant, a good wedding planner who will follow your orders and take charge of the party on your wedding day. Look for small touches which will make your party distinctive, but don't be afraid to think smaller. You don't need to have everything the bridal magazines say is a must. You need to choose your own priorities. The celebration of a marriage can be made as exciting and festive by investing imagination as by infusing cash.

I understand that the image of the white wedding, the desire to have a traditional cer-emony, is strong. I am not urging you to desert what you think make you and your guests comfortable; but even if you want the conventional white wedding and dinner dance, there are still ways to make your wedding distinctive, to break away from the formulas which caterers and wedding planners will tell you are the only choices. I don't admire oddball weddings. What I do admire is a beautiful wedding with distinctive touches that make everything seem personal. Like a monogram, a few well placed accents change an off-the-shelf style into a custom-tailored choice.

How then to create a party that celebrates who you are?

Play With Traditions

I think the party and the ceremony should both tell a story. Just as a ceremony cel-ebrates a new couple within a community of family, and friends, and neighbors, so the reason to have a reception and party is to include people. I see that impulse in the eating, drinking, music, and dancing that is a worldwide accompaniment to a wedding. Of course, exuberance comes from joy for the new couple. At some point during the party, most of us will want to have some formal time for the first dance, toasts, speeches, and a cake cutting. These forms of praise are akin to magic spells. Like the breaking of glasses against the wall, much of the noise and laughter of a wedding party was calculated to scare off evil spirits. Why not play with the traditions? For instance, the wedding cake comes from a tradition of fertility. In ancient times, a cake or loaf of bread (the staff of life) was broken over the bride's head to ensure fertility. In renaissance times, refined sugar was a rare commodity. White sugar icing was put on the cake as a sign of affluence and prosperity. In Victorian times, the tiered cake became popular along with baking techniques to support the weight of multiple tiers. Thus evolved the wedding cake which now can cost several hundred dollars. Keep the wedding cake; change the recipe. I have always appreciated the surprise of cupcakes and cream-puff cakes, carrot and spice cakes, and homemade cakes which offer a reminiscence of the days when weddings really happened in the front parlor. Even an elegant cake from a high-end baker need not be a tower. One of the prettiest cakes I've seen was a simple two-layer circle with a bouquet arrangement in its center. This couple used a sheath of wheat bound with ribbons recalling the origins of the cake tradition. Tradition evolves from symbolism, superstition, and prestige. With understanding of its origins, however, tradition can continue to evolve to reflect modern attitudes and realities.

Set the Scene

My favorite weddings occur in beautiful locations. Certainly many catering halls offer gardens. I don't favor garden weddings unless one can control the weather. If you want a garden wedding, plan on spring and autumn when the weather tends to be temperate. Check the location at the same time of day you plan to have the ceremony. Is it in full sun or well-shaded? Be sure to have fans and water for everyone. I remember one particularly gruesome August event held in a garden modeled after Versailles. The rehearsal day brought 105-degree heat. The caterer suggested we rehearse indoors, but the bride, fearing that an indoor rehearsal would lead to an indoor ceremony on the next day (and she was probably right), insisted we troop out to the pergola to practice. We successfully completed our work, and, as we stood in the heat, one of the bridesmaids keeled over. The EMS had to be called. Luckily, a bottle of Gatorade cured her heat prostration, and all was well…until the next day when the cold front arrived and violent thunderstorms struck. We ended up indoors. Disappointing? A little; but the ceremony was lovely because the *words had been individualized*.

Gardens

The garden goes back to the story of Eden. At a wedding, the couple is, in a sense, the first man and the first woman. The ritual of a ceremony should make us stop and look with wonder that life is always renewing, and humanity is always starting again. A garden is more than flowers. The rich tradition of the green man is found worldwide and includes in its fertility images an abundance of fruits and vegetables. Vines, grasses and leaves as well as flowers can be used to create a decorative story of the life force celebrated at a wedding. If you are making a garden wedding, consider how the setting can be used as more than a backdrop. Have the guests bring a flower forward to create a backdrop of blossoms for the ceremony by placing the bloom in a container that sits at the rear of the ceremonial space. Have seed packets or small container plants as favors so that the guests can go home and plant their own gardens.

The Japanese say that a perfect garden has all the elements of the world — earth, sky, air, and water. Not all gardens are equal. If you want a garden wedding, look for a location that is more than out of doors. Do you have a local historic house that is available for parties? Is there a botanical garden or park which provides facilities for a party? These gardens often have fuller perennial plantings and century-old trees. In the New York City area, the Hudson Valley provides a spectacular assortment of outdoor sites with views of the river. The ultimate garden wedding is framed by trees and flowers with a sublime view of water and hills as a backdrop. This can be pricey, but look around your area. A little exploration and imagination can pay off. One of the most elegant weddings I ever attended was at a small Italian restaurant with a large patio overlooking a pond. Lovely tablecloths, candles and white roses transformed the mom–and-pop place into a trattoria. Floating candles were launched just before the ceremony which was timed with sunset. As the evening approached, the flickering flames played with the golden light, creating a memorable setting for the launching of a new marriage.

Your Own Backyard

Even a suburban backyard can be turned into a spectacular setting for a wedding. One of my friends transformed his prosaic yard by completely tenting it over with a clear plastic roof. Colored spotlights were hung in the trees which brushed against the tent top, and white fairy lights were braided around tent poles and entrances. As evening came, the effect made the guests feel as if we were in a magical tree house. Some of my couples have also cherished the significance of having guests come to their new home for their wedding. Returning to the tradition of the parlor wedding, they made home and family the theme of the party. They have changed their backyard by investing it with high spirits: long tables with checkered tablecloths, and a country band, and a caller; ragtime music and kazoos for joining in; strolling musicians playing ethnic and old-time favorites. An outdoor wedding when the weather cooperates is an invitation to enjoy more than a ceremony in the sun. Ask yourself what the setting symbolizes for your life together.

Where else can you find the four elements of a garden? Sometimes not in a garden at all. An acquaintance in Sydney, Australia, performs ceremonies in a helicopter over the harbor. Air, earth, sky and water. I think of this as a stunt wedding, but a setting that is extreme for me is spectacular to someone else. I am always moved by the extraordinary views of the Statue of Liberty and New York Harbor which have been the back drop to some of my weddings. One of my favorite couples was married at a lovely restaurant in New York's Battery Park. The flowers and food were opulent, but I was moved by the view of Miss Liberty and Ellis Island, and the story they told of great grandparents who had landed here 100 years before and whose descendants now enjoyed such luxury.

A Bower of Ribbons

Sometimes an industrial space holds an unappreciated treasure. One couple whose parents came from China and South America used a factory loft for their wedding. The loft's windows stretched 180 degrees around three sides of the massive, empty space. One could look from the George Washington Bridge at one end of Manhattan to the Statue of Liberty at the other end of the harbor. Rather than clutter the space with chairs, low banquettes provided seating islands for the ceremony and the ensuing reception. With a path of rose petals winding through the room, we felt like we were in a garden with a view that stretched to the horizon. A bower of red ribbons echoed the color of the flowers scattered across the room, defining the ceremonial space. Red ribbons were then used during the ceremony as guests from all over the world presented them to the couple as a symbol of binding their two lives together. Below and around us, the lights of New York with their excitement and glamour made their own testimony to the international story of this couple's love. The setting became a sparkling fairy garden as evening arrived.

A Country Feast

I am happy to say, I even follow my own advice. The adage is that the shoemaker's children have no shoes, but when the time came for my own son's wedding, he and his wife chose a 19th-century factory building that had been turned into a museum of technology and industry. A small, rural museum, the rental was minimal. The ceremony was set beside a waterfall and creek in the meadow behind the museum. The New England charm of the mill run and the surrounding woods appealed to them. The bride and groom wanted to emerge from the forest (echoes of the green-man tradition). The groomsmen held a canopy over the couple's head, and the guests stood in the forest clearing except for those who needed chairs because of age or disability. When the party moved inside, the museum building provided drama with tall ceilings and large open rooms, as well as wonderful glass cabinets filled with tools and gears. Who would have thought that machinery is beautiful, but the antique gears and wheels on display were like a gallery of folk art.

We decided to follow the style of the space by creating the ultimate country picnic. We provided an elegant country feast with artisanal bread and cheese as well as charcuterie and pâté. We invited family and friends to bake a specialty cookie for dessert, supplemented by heirloom pies. We decorated white cardboard picnic boxes with stamped designs and gave them to the guests as favors; everyone filled the boxes with leftovers and took home some of the sweetness of the day. We created that wedding on a very modest budget. Many government and nonprofit organizations try to make income from renting their spaces. Often an alternative space can be had for the cost of covering the insurance. My sister-in-law rented a park pavilion from the State of New York. A friend used a boat house in a local New Jersey park. Another couple used the amphitheater of their local high school, and colleges often have hidden landscape and architectural treasures on their campuses.

Art

For those with the means, art museums often open their galleries to parties. One of my couples made their vows in a classical courtyard of columns and fountains. The party took place in the great hall of the museum mansion, with centerpiece reproductions of Greek vases and statuary. Old department stores often offer similar settings as they were designed as temples of commerce. Some of the most delightful and colorful spaces I have seen are in children's museums and sculpture gardens. Perhaps the most spectacular example of the latter is in Seattle, where the new downtown sculpture walk combines views of Puget Sound with monumental, outdoor sculpture by leading 20th-century artists.

Setting a wedding in the midst of art tells the story of new perspectives and wonderful transformations. A wedding is a celebration of creativity and hope. Setting the celebration in a space filled with objects that transmit these expressions is a powerful accent to the story of a marriage. Some of my clients have used art even more powerfully by commissioning a piece of art or a performance for their wedding. We think of such gestures as the province of the rich and powerful, but a modest budget can often hire a wonderful musician or dancer from the local college to create a command performance. I have been delighted at a wedding with processional and recessional fanfares created by local brass players. I vividly remember a dance company from a local school making a wedding night special with a performance of tango. I have used remarkable singers who are studying opera to sing for a ceremony and, then, to do a tribute performance during dinner. There are so many talented people in our communities who are delighted to have their work valued; if you truly want to be a king and a queen for a day, create a command performance.

Stretch Your Imagination —
Programs and Menus

Imagination is a muscle. The more you exercise, the more ideas will come. The emotion and excitement of a wedding often feel overwhelming, but start small, and start early, and ideas will come. Small considerations make big statements. Consider details like your program. On warm summer evenings, I often see guests using their program to cool themselves. If you are outside, consider printing the program on a fan. Your guest will both read it and keep it. One of the most beautiful programs I have seen was printed as a book with different-colored pages. It included the evening's schedule, the order of the ceremony and the text of the readings, the menu for the reception and dinner, the list of the wedding party and a thank you to all the guests for attending. The piece was so pretty, it became a keepsake on its own. The bride designed it and took it to Staples to be collated. Computers and printer technology give everyone the access to individual choices. Even if you can't realize the final piece, create a prototype and bring it to a print store. People are often so happy to have a special project that they will go out of their way to help you realize the final product.

Wedding menus seem to have nothing but the usual beef, chicken and fish as alternatives. When planning your menu, look in food magazines for ideas that can enhance the conventional main course. Why not make substitutions like a pear-walnut salad with gorgonzola instead of a tossed salad; or polenta instead of potatoes. Look at regional and ethnic specialties to make a menu fun. A variation from the usual string beans and potatoes can make a plain plate special. Consider Chinese dumplings, arepas and tamales, Middle-Eastern meat and spinach pies. If you are working with a caterer, look at what he offers as an appetizer, and consider if something might become a main course. Short ribs and fried chicken can be a lot more satisfying than roast beef and salmon.

I am very much a foodie and love surprises. If you aren't locked into the necessity of a catering hall, think of the home cooking that regional and ethnic traditions can supply at local restaurants. You will receive incredible enthusiasm when you say you are considering having their food at your wedding. I enjoyed the backyard wedding where a local Indian restaurant set up a dosa grill supplying pancakes and spices. My friends from Australia invited us all to celebrate their wedding with an elegant Chinese banquet. My niece and nephew used a friend's Japanese restaurant for their wedding, getting the benefit of both the lovely garden and the top-quality sushi and sashimi. I have enjoyed beach weddings without shoes where dinner was a clam bake. One of my client couples used their international travels as a theme for their wedding, serving wonderful treats from Egypt, and Persia, and Turkey. My friend in the Smokey Mountains had pulled pork and square dancing. I believe a banquet feast can be made from really good handmade sausage, home-rolled gnocci and sauce, fresh-baked rolls, and salads. Be true to yourself and recognize that the occasion is about love, and the wedding feast prepared with love will far outshine a standardized meal whose ingredients came from a restaurant supply company.

Speak Up for Yourself

The natural impulse is to let an authority take charge. Everyone with whom you deal (including me) will consider himself an authority. Truthfully, we all have favorites, and we all have agendas. Remember, your once in a lifetime is a routine to the merchants and service providers who are servicing your ceremony and party. They will suggest solutions that will avoid problems, ease their job, and profit their bottom line. They are

THE HEART OF THE WEDDING

experienced, but don't be afraid to exercise your imaginations. Within their well-polished formulas, room remains to add details that will make your ceremony and party unique.

Your Table

Consider table settings and decoration. I once performed a ceremony in a 19th-century college dining hall that had a large pipe organ at one end and huge paned windows running down one side. The space was unique, but a bit overpowering, and potentially institutional. The bride had sheer golden slip covers placed on the plain straight-back chairs and turned them into little thrones. The ivory tablecloths were overlaid with a gossamer bolt of golden voile. The dishes were a deep red-clay color, and the centerpieces were red and cream roses surrounded with small votive candles. The theatricality of the colors transformed the space into a royal castle. Don't be afraid of color. The rich tones of a tablecloth can increase the impact of your table setting and make a common room special. You will need to rent tablecloths. As long as you are spending the money, use them to effect.

A unique centerpiece also helps to create a well-dressed table. Flowers belong at weddings, but I have often wondered at the expense of flowers. I am delighted by beautiful bouquets, but many ways exist to use flowers lavishly without spending a fortune. Sometimes less is more. Think Japanese. Instead of making a great display of blossoms, highlight one or two beautiful flowers floating in a bowl of water and colored stones, or place a stem of orchids or a charming Gerbera daisy across each place setting, or as a flower chain in the table's center. Avoid tall arrangements. It is better to see who is sitting across the table. Think low and colorful. Go to your local garden store and get pots of annuals, impatiens, mums, and daisies to cluster at the center of your table. One of the most striking table settings I ever saw bunched votive candles into the center as a sparkling highlight, and white and purple stem orchids in a bud vase at each place setting as a favor. Everyone got to take home flowers. Think alternatively, and use design to make a statement. I have seen grasses and branches, stones and shells, used to create a centerpiece. One of my favorite weddings had golden tablecloths with orange pumpkins and autumn leaves as decoration. Perhaps the most theatrical centerpiece I ever saw was at a Russian nightclub in Brooklyn. I don't have the technical explanation of how it occurred, but as I pronounced the couple husband and wife, the centerpieces exploded in fireworks.

Flowers and Decorations

Finding a good florist is a job. The average cost of flowers at a wedding is $1,500. They are selling you flowers. You want to consider effect. Even for the ceremony, I believe that less is more. Instead of huge bouquets framing the bride and groom (they only get in the way of the wedding party), consider making an aisle of flower petals: my favorite. I dislike the paper rolls some florists foist on brides who wish to walk on a white carpet.

The paper usually wrinkles and, often, catches people's heels. Instead, make a thick line of rose petals with a small bouquet of roses placed strategically along the path of the bridal party. The flower girl can sprinkle more petals for the bride to walk upon, if you so choose. Place a bouquet of several dozen roses up front to frame the ceremony. The mass of flowers will make a beautiful effect. Often, you can get a better price if you buy a large quantity of the same flower. Masses of the same blossom will give you a feeling of opulence.

Also consider using swags of cloth to frame your ceremony. I have seen Indian saris and sheer curtains from the thrift store transformed into pillars of gold and silver when woven and draped on a simple trellis. The Jews have a tradition of standing under a prayer shawl when they marry. Interpolate on this age-old symbol which suggests the dome of heaven and the roof of the new household. Enclose blank sheets of colored papers with your invitation and ask the guests to send back a wish or a blessing. Then staple these wishes to a large square of cloth. Use the colorful patchwork as a bower of blessings under which to say your vows. You can hang it as a tent, or have four groomsmen hold the bower above the heads of the bride and groom as would be done at a Jewish wedding.

With the tool of the Internet, you can find wonderful items to use for decoration. I have seen couples use lanterns, Mylar streamers, and strings of lights for their wedding bower. I have even seen projections used so that virtual images decorated a screen behind the ceremony. If you have Photoshop, you can create a montage of family pictures and project it as your backdrop. Make an evocative light show, using colors and images to tell your story much as a theater director uses lighting and sound design to heighten the emotion of her production. Ritual is the origin of theater. Don't be afraid to brainstorm and think theatrically. Use images to tell your story. One of my couples had a wonderful story of coming home to rebuild a house together. At the end of their ceremony they released a flight of doves, bearing our wishes and cheers up into the sky and down the road back home. (It happened that the roost to which the doves returned was just down the road from the couple's home. A nice coincidence, but symbols don't have to be literal.) Another couple told a love story of renewal and discovery by releasing butterflies at the end of their ceremony in a magical moment of innocence and hope.

Integrate Music into the Ceremony

Music belongs at a wedding and is a strong part of the design. The deejay usually considers the ceremony an afterthought; but when I officiated at a Latino (I mention this not because it is a common cultural phenomenon, but because the music offered was Latin) wedding five years ago, the deejay had read the ceremony which I had written and had prepared music to play under each section. I felt like I was in a film with a soundtrack, the music augmenting my words and images. My experience as a performer served me well, and this deejay was an excellent sound designer. Not every officiant would be able to incorporate an element like music into the ceremony, but that experience taught me the power of having music throughout. So when a couple asked me to create a ceremony for them using the cabaret piano in their space, I eagerly found song lyrics that would serve as readings. We spoke the words, but the music ran underneath. Instead of Bach and Mendelssohn, we had Nat King Cole and Frank Sinatra. It was more meaningful because the couple met to the sound of these songs. Instead of the traditional wedding march, consider drums, klezmer sounds, or jazz. Find the music that reflects who you are and weave it into your ceremony.

Don't forget, if you have the chance, use *acoustic instruments.* I believe the sound of music being made without amplification carries far more emotion than electronically amplified sound. I love the sound of a classical guitar or a harp announcing the bride. When a string quartet plays the Beatles, the music is lyrical and romantic. I performed a ceremony at a country inn with a banjo player strumming as the guests arrived. He then led them into the ceremony where he changed instruments, playing the mandolin for the processional and recessional themes. Bagpipes are another traditional accompaniment to weddings — especially wonderful out of doors! I fondly recall the bagpiper who summoned us all forth and led us over a rise to meet the wedding couple who awaited us in a forest glade. I have been moved and delighted by the sound of horns, and I don't think there is anything so wonderful as a good singer a capella. Local colleges have faculty and students who provide a rich resource for acoustic musicians.

Appreciate the Small Gesture

Finally, a wedding should have a quality of sublimity — a moment when the ordinary becomes extraordinary, and when emotion makes us see our place in a far greater pattern. Edmund Burke, the great British critic, wrote an essay on the sublime. He described the juxtaposition of images which contrast the great power of history and nature with the ephemeral moment of the individual. He wrote of the emotions which produce awe, the recognition of the finite within the striving to discover the infinite. The memorable moment of a wedding is this personal statement of who you are, and why you have asked your guests to come. This moment becomes sublime because we all carry within us the memory of the collective, the great common repetition of the life passages which connect humanity across time and culture. The celebration of a wedding is one of the moments when we pause and recognize the sublime. Your ceremony should reflect that sensibility.

I think one of the elements most often left out of the celebration is a moment of silent recognition. I have written in this chapter of all the sensory stimuli which produce pleasure. As you plan your ceremony, also appreciate quiet gestures. At the opening of the ceremony, take a moment and hold hands, and when the party ends, consider a final dance of the bride and groom. The custom of giving guests a small wedding favor acknowledges that they are valued as a part of the wedding couple's community. I was very impressed when I saw a bride write a note to each of her guests to enclose with the favors. Most favors are ultimately superfluous, but the quiet expression of sentiment was a true treasure and a great gift.

Magical Time

Seventy years ago most people would have had their wedding in the front parlor. Times change, but the impulse to invite your guests into your life should remain. In the last decade, some couples have started to organize destination weddings. A few intimate guests are invited to come away to a beautiful location for several days to witness and be a part of the new couple's transformation. "Stay with us, be with us" becomes the message. Although not everyone is lucky enough to have the option of going to an exotic beach to be married, the image is appropriate. Your party should be a retreat from everyday time to magical time. Time is stopped by sentiment, that moment of aha! Those instances when we all breathe together in recognition of the universality of our need to be a family. Ultimately, a great party must start with a great ceremony. Find an officiant who will tell your story, who will use his/her knowledge of ritual structure to include your family and friends with heart-filled images and words, and who will send you home to begin the rest of your life with the full sense of the threshold you have just crossed together. Don't dismiss the ceremony as a prelude to the party.

Your wedding is a moment of becoming one, an experience of alchemy in which the common event of another marriage becomes the gold of your marriage. Find someone whose words catch the magic that starts the night. Ultimately, a wedding night is a celebration of the power of words. Make them all that they should be. Nothing can go wrong at a wedding as long as the words are true. Laugh, cry, remember those who are gone, and look to the future with words that belong to you.

I offer you all of these suggestions, but, ultimately, no one should tell you what is right for you. Listen, take what suits, and do what expresses who you are. There are no wedding police, and there should be none. This is your moment.

Celebrate.

Chapter Ten

DOING IT FOR YOURSELF

Whatever size or design your wedding party takes, you want your wedding ceremony to be the heart of the celebration. Long after you have forgotten the wine, and food, and music, you will remember the words you have said to each other. This chapter lays out techniques for collecting your own stories, setting objectives for your ceremony, and discovering the core images that create the spine of the ceremony. Here, I explain ceremonial structure and discuss how to find your unique voice while using resources from the Internet and from literature.

First, let's set priorities.

As couples start to plan their weddings, they usually ask each other three questions:

1. How many guests?
2. Formal or informal?
3. Traditional or non-traditonal?

I THINK THE FIRST QUESTION SHOULD BE, WHO'S WRITING AND SHAPING THE CEREMONY? I believe that the choice to have a wedding celebration is inherently a decision to be inclusive — not just to have family, friends and acquaintances present, but to include them in a moment of your life that will forever prove a bond between you and them. One can get married with a stranger as a witness and an Elvis impersonator as an officiant, but once you decide to offer invitations to family and friends, the first task becomes choosing who and how many to include as witnesses and participants. I have been to ceremonies of 250 and more. The bride and groom claim that everyone is special to them. "I have a large family" is a common statement and, often, the truth. When invitations go out, it's very easy to add up the couples two by two. If this parallels your circumstance, however many guests are present, the ceremony must be written and performed so that each guest feels included from the front row to the 24th row.

The objective should be to make all in attendance feel their full presence is important. Everyone should be listening, involved aurally and emotionally, and not staring at
their watch and waiting for the big party to begin. On the other hand, I have been to
receptions with no one but a half dozen friends and family. Strangely, the intimacy of
such a situation can encourage a feeling of casualness. The couple and their guests might
mistakenly feel that size connotes informality and insignificance. "I want something
short and simple," clients sometimes say to me. "We don't care about the words. Its only
six people." In fact, everyone present should feel privileged to participate in this transformative ritual, and the bride and groom should feel empowered to speak their hearts
to each other. True intimacy and emotional vulnerability is unforgettable and becomes a
foundation for the rest of your lives.

I recently officiated at a wedding at an upscale Park Avenue hotel. The couple had
come from out of town and hired a stylist to arrange the wedding. The stylist and a
member of the hotel staff were the witnesses for the ceremony. The room for the ceremony had been emptied of furniture and decorated with a simple, but elegant, bouquet
of roses standing on a table by the window. A path of rose petals led into a circle of petals
that defined the ceremonial space. At the couple's request, we began the ceremony by
leaving them alone. The bride entered, and we all exited. After two minutes, we re-
entered. I wonder what words the almost husband and wife said to each other. Or did
they simply stand silently and together look out the window at the life that awaited them?
Did they touch? I think not. I think (and I must admit, it took professional discipline not
to listen at the keyhole) they simply shared that space as they were about to share their
lives. They stood with each other and breathed. A wedding is so much about breath, the
symbol of life. A kiss is a shared breath. In the Bible, God breathed life into Adam. Lao
Tzu connects breath with the creation of the physical world. Hindu yogis use breath to
attain higher consciousness. Breath energizes and refreshes and enlivens.

When I entered the room after the agreed upon interval, I found the couple facing
each other in the circle of rose petals. I asked them to take each other's hands and con-
template the future they were now about to share. I asked the witnesses to observe that
today these two people had asked us to hear them vow to live as husband and wife. I
then read the monitum. The monitum is a warning that this vow is, indeed, a binding
agreement to the exclusion of all others, and entered into with the full intention that this
marriage will last for the rest of the bride and groom's life. I then asked the couple if they
agreed to take each other to be husband and wife. They replied "I do." Technically, this
affirmation is all the witnesses have to hear. I did ask the couple to repeat the traditional
vows after me.

I think these words have meaning, and I enjoy the tradition of saying them. The couple then exchanged rings, and I pronounced them husband and wife. This ceremony may have lasted five minutes including the two minutes of silence during which I stood outside the door. It was probably the most intense ceremony I had ever attended. I think we will all remember the intimacy and truth of these few minutes. Each word was carefully attended. The choice of extreme simplicity became an elegant style to reflect the moment's eternal truth. I think of this ceremony as a haiku:

A man and woman
Finding their soul in each other
Share hearts and promise.

This ceremony's extreme simplicity showed me again that less can be more. I also realize that few couples would be comfortable emotionally or stylistically with the meditative quality of this ceremony. A wedding ritual must be constructed to move the participants, including the bride and groom, into the eternal truths from the mundane world. Most of us need help moving.

I recently did a ceremony for the son of a friend. We have lovely county parks in Essex County, New Jersey, designed by Frederick Law Olmstead, perhaps America's greatest landscape architect. The couple chose an idyllic setting by an old boathouse and lake. The ceremony took place on the steps of an arching stone bridge. Around us, children were playing soccer, families were walking their dogs, elderly men were arriving to fish. I asked the guests to follow me to the bridge. I encouraged them to move in tighter to the steps. When all were gathered, I read one of my favorite poems by the great Cuban poet Jose Marti.

Love is born
With the pleasure of looking at each other.
It is fed
With the necessity of seeing each other.
It is concluded with the impossibility
Of ever being apart.

The bride and groom then joined our company by coming over the bridge towards us as if coming hand-in-hand over the horizon. Soccer, dogs, and fishing, were no longer present in our magic circle. The rest of the world had stopped as we all looked at this young couple walking into their new life together. Even pedestrian passers-by felt the power of the ritual circle and, while curious and excited to see a wedding, held back some 10 feet or so, respecting our space.

Whatever the size of your wedding, whatever the style, the ceremony starts with the processional. The processional creates the transformational circle in which one's life is changed. I urge my clients to do a rehearsal for this reason (and don't feel you must do it the way the caterer tells you it should be done. In fact, even in the most formal white weddings, the processional can have variations.) The processional tells the story of the couple's changing status from single to married. I officiated at an Albanian wedding with 16 bridesmaids and an equal number of groomsmen, which presented me with a logistical problem of where to have everyone stand. Symbolically, however, the picture of the mass of young people launching their peers into full adulthood resonated with a sense of long-ago tradition. Many of the older women wore Muslim headscarves. I do have a romantic imagination, and I could not help but imagine the ancient village where all the young people would go to gather the bride and groom and proceed with them to the ceremony.

So, with flexibility, set your priorities on size and style; but whatever your choices, remember that the ceremony is telling your story, and should do so with imagination and feeling from the moment the guests are seated.

How to define your story?

Too many clients come to me claiming that they have no story. Our culture makes us feel inadequate if we cannot match the intricacies of a Hollywood scriptwriter's mind. Nonsense. Everyone has the greatest story — YOU ARE GOING TO GET MARRIED.

Don't take it for granted. Marriage is an adventure which involves an enormous leap of faith. Butch and Sundance hold hands as they leap off the cliff into the raging rapids. Thelma and Louise in their Thunderbird convertible are together forever as they race over the edge of the Grand Canyon. Hollywood reserves the best images for buddy movies; but truth is, when you get married, you leap over the edge. Why not hold hands?

Your story is the leap that you are taking together. Begin with the symbolic statement that you are not afraid as long as you are figuratively holding hands. Traditionally, a priest might perform a blessing, even tie hands together. Jews raise a wedding canopy or chupah over the bride and groom to signify the sacred space they will now fill as a couple. I always remember the couple who asked all the guests to hold hands. We then asked them to avow their support of this couple's marriage by shouting "WE DO!" The unity candle is a modern (1980s) symbolic variation. What a way to reach out to each other. Two flames become one. Most of us would be too terrified to do so, but I have had couples sing a love duet to each other. Exhilarating!

Have the officiant tell how you decided to marry.

Most people find this last task incredibly hard to do. They get lost in the details. They tell too much. I do not mean to have a complete chronology of your time together. Choose one moment that will become the image of your relationship. I ask my clients to tell me a funny story that happened to them. Often it will contain the image that we need — the old gnarled tree that leans in the field behind the house; losing the trail on a hike and soaking in a thermal spring; or a favorite family saying.

Use that image as a destination for your story, the lesson of why you marry.

Thus, I described Gretchen and John's marriage with their story of being directionally disabled, the classic tale of the wrong road leading you to adventure and reward.

John told me of one hike near Hot Springs which took hours and miles longer than it should have. He said, "The hike tallied twice the miles on our feet that it really should have. BUT along the journey we saw many wonderful creatures and marveled at the beauteous flora peaking out of its wintery hibernation; but the nicest thing we came across was the soaking of soreness out of our exhausted bones in the blissful peace of our own private hot spring." Life is like that — sometimes we lose the path, but if we have a trusted partner we don't panic. Instead we use the opportunity for discovery, and eventually, get home to soak our weary bones. When you are Gretchen and John, being lost is quickly turned into adventure; confusion becomes a reason for laughter, and each other's company makes a hard walk easier.

Writing your story means thinking symbolically. Ritual is a right-brain activity: intuitive and holistic. A ceremony uses the left-hemisphere talents of structure and sequence to open our hearts to frame ritual, and within the ritual structure we are always reviving the symbolic images of the life passage taking place, and the universal story being told. Thus, Gretchen and John's hikes became the path they will tread together. The story of their mishaps becomes the lesson of sharing.

When Alex and Richard built their new home, they chose its location because of a magnificent tree. Building a new home is a daunting experience for anyone, and even more so for a couple just being married. They never imagined how much tension a door knob could generate. But that tree was the tree of life — their symbol of the power that time and life will bring when a marriage is well-rooted.

I wrote:

Unbalanced and imperfect yet majestic and striking, its great branches rise up to the sky in celebration. Tonight, we share with Alexandra and Richard this season when their lives will change, when two will become one in a new pattern of life, as two trees deeply rooted in separate plots of ground reach up and out, forming a miracle of lace against the heavens.

Angelo and Donna's love grew so seamlessly, there was never a necessity for a formal proposal. They both thought they would never marry again; but one day, Angelo said, "I want to grow old with you," and they began planning a wedding. The realization was like a reawakening of hopes and dreams that they both thought they would never see again. I used one of Angelo's favorite proverbs.

A $50 piece and a $20 piece have the same exact value at the bottom of the lake...it's when you bring out and use what's hidden that you realize the value. Donna and Angelo, you have found in each other a treasure of love that will now enrich and sustain your lives, come what may.

Donna and Angelo's story paralleled the folktale of the treasure hidden in the dark corner where we always look, but never see. If we could only look closer, we will discover the hidden value that lies within reach. There are countless tales which tell how we search the world for the treasure of our dreams, only to find it hidden under our own hearth, or within the roots of the tree by our own front door. The old stories echo our life stories, and if you wish to write your own ceremony, look to the truth of the symbols which lie in the commonplace. The garden, the road, the piper, the magic ring, transformation and transcendence are the stuff of stories, and the story we tell at weddings.

The more we think with our left brain, the clearer we see the messages that the old stories bring.

A good story needs action.

Ritual has a purpose in all ceremony. If I tell a story about blueberry pancakes on Sunday morning, and picnic baskets packed on the rear hood of a red Triumph, I am setting the images and emotions of my story. But I need my story to go somewhere, to have those images transform into the universal. Ritual is the transformational tool. Don't think of ritual as being just candles and incense. Ritual can include a reading, a song, a symbolic use of objects, a procession or dance, a slide show Powerpoint production, any physical representation of the symbolic story we are telling. Blueberry pancakes aren't just milk, eggs, and flour; they are the stuff of life. And the flashy little sports car is the coach setting out on the magic road of adventure. The ritual we need for this story should be a sending forth, and so we choose to have the bride's mother read the childhood Dr. Seuss poem "Oh! The Places You'll Go." Poetry's rhythms and rhymes alter our brain patterns. While some may feel that Dr. Seuss is too silly for a wedding, in fact, the images of the poem were exactly what this wedding was about — two people setting off to discover the world. Asking the bride's mother to read offered the power of a parent's blessing. The poem, an iconographic piece of American children's literature, had special meaning to three generations of this family who have shared it mother to daughter. Ritual does not have to be pompous to be powerful. It has to be truthful.

An aspect of ritual is that it reorders time and makes the impossible happen. Past, present and future all collapse into the heightened moment. A candle is lit, special language is read, a flame is passed, and suddenly the image, the words, and the feelings all tell the story that the spark of life moves and sustains from generation to generation. As you create your ceremony, take the time to do what you want. If you are carrying your story into the universal, time will wait. I have had wedding couples who wanted a set of grandparents, two sets of parents and all 12 members of the wedding party to light a candle at the opening of the ceremony. The image created was a tabletop of light. Beautiful! We set up a surface of votive candles. We chose a soft, lyrical piece of music to play under my words, called each participant up by name, read a sentence or two about the special place each holds in the couple's history. The procession of participants became a wonderful compilation of the couple's story as well as a pleasant display of music and movement. Don't fear movement as a part of the ceremony. Sometimes, the excuse is time. Sometimes, the excuse is someone will fall. Sometimes the excuse is that the idea of having family and friends stand up is too embarrassing. The purpose of a wedding is to have your community "stand up and witness" the connection being forged between these two loving humans. Physicalizing the purpose of the ceremony is entirely appropriate. People neither trip nor make fools of themselves. They take the honor of being included so seriously they will remember the moment for the rest of their lives. In truth, the only reservation from either side is the shyness our culture imposes on us when we see a display of feeling. "I'll cry," I'm often told; to which I reply, "Weddings are the time for laughter and tears. Nothing makes a wedding more memorable than feelings truthfully felt." In fact, the physicalization of ritual imposes structure on emotion, giving the tears and laughter a frame that tells the story, reinforces the value, and gives everyone permission to accept and rejoice in the mixture of emotion.

To do it yourself

1. **Separately, make a timeline from first meeting (even if it was in kindergarten) to present.** On this timeline mark significant moments, memorable stories, odd coincidences, missed opportunities, treasured memories. Compare your timelines and as you do so, tell your stories. Note which events were on both timelines. Choose the shared moment that was most symbolic of the couple you have become.

2. **Separately, write your own version of this story.** If this wasn't your favorite story on the timeline, write your version of that favorite moment of your relationship. Compare your versions. What are these stories about? Can you identify the parallels to a traditional motif? Was there a path not taken, a card not dealt, a treasure overlooked, a little bird ignored, or was there a moment when the gates opened, the spell was broken, and the magic was revealed? I remember a wonderful story of a bride who met her intended and said, "I love short, Jewish guys with glasses who play video games." The potential groom (who was a short, Jewish guy with glasses who played video games) thought to himself, "Damn, I wish it were me." Obviously, this is a variation of the frog prince. The romantic prince emerged finally several months later, when, after not seeing each other in weeks, the groom called to ask if he could come over. He arrived with flowers and a passionate kiss; and from that day on, the relationship flowered.

3. **Name the objective of ritual which parallels the story.** The above example was a story about transformation. We used a shared wine glass to follow the story. Wine is transformational, changing us. By the sharing of wine, the bride and groom are connected to the universal and changed. We bless them, "May all that you are always be in love. May all that is love always be in you."

4. **Choose a reading that tells this same story in a different way.** Roy Croft's classic love poem echoes the discovery of the real person inside.

   I love you
   For putting your hand
   Into my heaped-up heart
   And passing over
   All the foolish, weak things
   That you can't help
   Dimly seeing there,
   And for drawing out
   Into the light
   All the beautiful belongings
   That no one else had looked
   Quite far enough to find

5. **You now have the core idea of your ceremony.** Create an outline of the beginning, middle and end: Procession; Handholding; Story and Ritual Connection; Reading; Monitum; Vows; Pronouncement.

6. **Under each section, begin to list your needs and desires.** The outline might look something like this:

Procession
Grandma and Ed
Mother of bride with Jack
4 groomsmen and groom
4 bridesmaids
bride and father

Handholding
Candle ceremony with parents and grandma

Story
Our crazy hike to nowhere

Ritual
Presentation of marker stones by family and friends — the path we have trod

Reading
ee cummings "i carry your heart (in my heart)"

Vows
For better for worse
My life and love are bound to you forever

Presentation
Mr. Frank Gaggiacia and Mrs. Edna Wills-Gaggiacia

7. **Begin looking for an officiant.** I am always surprised by the number of couples who call a week or two before their wedding date. Start your discussion with an officiant as soon as you set a wedding date. Discuss whether you want a religious service, a civil celebrant, or a judge. Sometimes the result will surprise you. The religious ceremony is engrained in the American culture. A friend of my son's came to me with his fiancée. I had known him since he was twelve and could not imagine anyone doing a more affectionate, intimate, and engaging ceremony than me. Three days later, John emailed, "I think we are going with a church wedding. I never realized how conservative I am until I discussed making this decision with you." The couple needed a religious context to understand the specialness of this moment.

I thought it was great that I had helped them realize what they wanted. I tell the couples who come to me to choose their officiant carefully. Many people of different points of view do wonderful ceremonies. Some, however, just say words. Choose the story you want to tell, and whoever you choose as an officiant will do a better job for having you discuss your story, and ritual, and reading ideas. If an officiant says, "I only do it this way" — as may be the case with a cleric — then you can choose if that is the way you want to go. As you choose your officiant, remember you will be looking at the person's face in your photos 20 years from now. Choose the person who you will remember because he or she is truly connected to you, not because the cost is $100 cheaper. Why do couples economize on their officiant when they are spending so much on the ephemeral flowers, wine and food of a party? YOUR CEREMONY IS THE HEART OF YOUR WEDDING. Make your choices for quality.

8. **Stay open and involved.** There are no wedding police. Write the ceremony and chose the ideas that make you celebrate with the whole range of emotions you are feeling on your wedding day. Don't give over because you feel that someone else knows better or because you feel overwhelmed. Think about your ceremony. Think about your stories. Consider who can voice the meaning of the day. Don't dismiss the personal voice to a toast at dinner. The deepest truths are said simply. Include a personal statement in the ceremony. My cousin Pearl is a retired elementary-school principal. Articulate and thoughtful, she was asked to be a part of her granddaughter's ceremony. She asked if, instead of doing a reading, she could offer her own advice to the young couple. I think she wrote a classic statement from grandma:

To be called upon to speak at this most important moment in the life of Alyson and Jose is deeply touching — and humbling. What can I add to the beauty and significance of this day?

Today is all about love. And I'm not going to change the subject.

So let me give you my advice about love. You won't be surprised that my thoughts relate to grammatical usage.

You may remember that you were taught — and perhaps have taught your students — that the active voice of a verb is preferable to the passive voice. To say "I read the book" rather than "the book was read by me" makes a stronger statement.

The verb "love" is no exception.

So that is the essence of my advice to you. The passive of "love" — to be loved — is good — it is comforting, reassuring, very pleasant — but the active — to love — that's what love is really all about. The joy of loving is in loving — the thrill, the excitement of feeling, expressing, giving love.

So our wish to you — and I speak also for Grandpa — to you, Alyson, our first grandchild — and the one who made us get married so you could call me "Bubbe," instead of "Grandpa's girlfriend" — and to you, Jose, who have made a very special place for yourself in our hearts — Our wish for you both is that you will continue to love one another — to love freely, generously, unconditionally, enthusiastically, passionately! — For a long and joyous lifetime!

What to Include?

Google has transformed our lives. Countless wedding sites can be surfed for poetry, vows, and style ideas. I have little patience for navigating the ads and the cookies, but the material is out there. I prefer to urge you to go to the library. Daily Messenger, one of the original Australian civil celebrants, has an excellent book *Ceremonies and Celebrations*. It is filled with readings for all occasions. I have certain favorites which I use often. Some of them are clichés, but often a reading is used over and over again because it says what has to be said. You will see many more readings and blessings sprinkled throughout the example ceremonies of this book, but here are a collection of my favorites.

An Anonymous Limerick
Sukey, you shall be my wife
And I will tell you why:
I have got a little pig,
And you have got a sty;
I have got a dun cow,
And you can make good cheese.
Sukey, will you marry me?
Say yes, if you please.

Apache blessing – Second Verse

Go now to your dwelling place to enter into the days of your togetherness
And may your days be good and long upon the earth.

Treat yourselves and each other with respect, and
remind yourselves often of what brought you together.
Give the highest priority to the tenderness,
gentleness and kindness that your connection deserves.
When frustration, difficulties and fear assail your relationship,
as they threaten all relationships at one time or another,
remember to focus on what is right between you,
not only the part which seems wrong.
In this way, you can ride out the storms when
clouds hide the face of the sun in your lives — remembering that
even if you lose sight of it for a moment, the sun is still there.
And if each of you takes responsibility for the quality of your
life together, it will be marked by abundance and delight.

Excerpt from "Rivers and Mountains" by John Ashbery

... And now we are both setting sail into the purplish evening.
I love it! This cruise can never last long enough for me.
…Ribbons are flung, ribbons of clouds, And the sun seems to be coming out.
But there have been so many false alarms…
No, its happening!
The storm is over, again the weather is fine and clear…

And the voyage? Its on!
Listen, everybody, the ship is starting,
I can hear its whistles roar!
We have just enough time to make it to the dock!

And full of laugher and tears,
We sidle once again with the other passengers.
The ground is heaving under foot. Is it the ship?
It could be the dock…
And with a great whoosh all the sails go up…
Into the secretive, vaporous night with all of us!
Into the unknown,
The unknown that loves us,
The great unknown!

From the Bhagavad Gita

Look to this day,
For it is life,
The very life of life.
In its brief course lie all the varieties
And realities of your existence;
The bliss of growths
The glory of action,
The splendor of beauty;
For yesterday is but a dream
And tomorrow is only a vision,
But today well lived makes
Every yesterday a dream of happiness
And every tomorrow a vision of hope.

"How Do I Love Thee?" By Elizabeth Barrett Browning

How do I love thee? Let me count the ways.
I love thee to the depth and breadth and height
My soul can reach, when feeling out of sight
For the ends of Being and ideal Grace.
I love thee to the level of every day's
Most quiet need, by sun and candle-light.
I love thee freely, as men strive for Right;
I love thee purely, as they turn from Praise.
I love thee with a passion put to use
In my old griefs, and with my childhood's faith.
I love thee with a love I seemed to lose
With my lost saints; — I love thee with the breath,
Smiles, tears, of all my life! — And, if God choose,
I shall but love thee better after death.

"A Red, Red Rose" by Robert Burns

O, my luve is like a red, red rose
That's newly sprung in June;
O, my luve's like the melodie
That's sweetly played in tune.

As fair thou art, my bonnie lass,
So deep in luve am I;
And I will luve thee still, my dear,
Till a' the seas gang dry.

Till a' the seas gang dry, my dear,
And the rocks melt wi' the sun;
I will luve thee still, my dear,
While the sands o' life shall run.

Excerpt from "From Beginning to End" by Robert Fulghum

You have known each other from the first glance of acquaintance to this point of commitment. At some point, you decided to marry. From that moment of yes to this moment of yes, indeed, you have been making promises and agreements in an informal way. All those conversations that were held riding in a car or over a meal or during long walks — all those sentences that began with "When we're married" and continued with "I will and you will and we will"- those late night talks that included "someday" and "somehow" and "maybe"- and all those promises that are unspoken matters of the heart. All these common things, and more, are the real process of a wedding. The symbolic vows that you are about to make are a way of saying to one another, " You know all those things we've promised and hoped and dreamed — well, I meant it all, every word." Look at one another and remember this moment in time. Before this moment you have been many things to one another — acquaintance, friend, companion, lover, dancing partner, and even teacher — for you have learned much from one another in these last few years. Now you shall say a few words that take you across a threshold of life, and things will never quite be the same between you. For after these vows, you shall say to the world, this — is my husband, this — is my wife.

Excerpt from "All I Really Need to Know I Learned in Kindergarten" by Robert Fulghum

*Most of what I really need to know about how to live and what to do and how to be
I learned in kindergarten ... Share Everything ... Play Fair ... Don't Hit People ...
Clean Up Your Own Mess ... Say You're Sorry When You Hurt Someone ... Live
A Balanced Life ... When You Go Out Into The World Watch Out For Traffic, Hold
Hands, And Stick Together.*

"On Love" by Thomas à Kempis

*Love is a mighty power, a great and complete good.
Love alone lightens every burden, and makes rough places smooth.
It bears every hardship as though it were nothing, and renders
all bitterness sweet and acceptable.
Nothing is sweeter than love, Nothing stronger,
Nothing higher, Nothing wider,
Nothing more pleasant,
Nothing fuller or better in heaven or earth; for love is born of God.
Love flies, runs and leaps for joy. It is free and unrestrained.
Love knows no limits, but ardently transcends all bounds.
Love feels no burden, takes no account of toil,
attempts things beyond its strength.
Love sees nothing as impossible, for it feels able to achieve all things.
It is strange and effective,
while those who lack love faint and fail.
Love is not fickle and sentimental, nor is it intent on vanities.
Like a living flame and a burning torch,
it surges upward and surely surmounts every obstacle.*

"Love" by Roy Croft

I love you,
Not only for what you are,
But for what I am
When I am with you.

I love you,
Not only for what
You have made of yourself,
But for what
You are making of me.

I love you
For the part of me
That you bring out;
I love you
For putting your hand
Into my heaped-up heart
And passing over
All the foolish, weak things
That you can't help Dimly seeing there,
And for drawing out
Into the light
All the beautiful belongings
That no one else had looked
Quite far enough to find.

I love you because you
Are helping me to make
Of the lumber of my life
Not a tavern
But a temple;
Out of the works
Of my every day
Not a reproach
But a song.

I love you
Because you have done
More than any creed
Could have done
To make me good,
And more than any fate
To make me happy.

You have done it
Without a touch,
Without a word,
Without a sign.
You have done it
By being yourself.

Perhaps that is what
Being in love means,
After all

"i carry your heart" by ee cummings

i carry your heart with me (i carry it in
my heart) i am never without it (anywhere
i go you go, my dear; and whatever is done by only me is your doing, my
darling)
i fear
no fate (for you are my fate, my sweet) i want
no world (for beautiful you are my world, my true)
and it's you are whatever a moon has always meant

and whatever a sun will always sing is you

here is the deepest secret nobody knows
(here is the root of the root and the bud of the bud
and the sky of the sky of a tree called life; which grows
higher than the soul can hope or mind can hide)
and this is the wonder that's keeping the stars apart

i carry your heart (i carry it in my heart)

"The Owl and The Pussy Cat" by Edward Lear

The Owl and the Pussycat went to sea
In a beautiful pea-green boat,
They took some honey, and plenty of money,
Wrapped up in a five pound note.
The Owl looked up to the stars above,
And sang to a small guitar,
"O lovely Pussy! O Pussy, my love,
What a beautiful Pussy you are, you are, you are,
What a beautiful Pussy you are."

Pussy said to the Owl
"You elegant fowl, How charmingly sweet you sing.
O let us be married, too long we have tarried;
But what shall we do for a ring?"
They sailed away, for a year and a day,
To the land where the Bong-tree grows,
And there in a wood a Piggy-wig stood
With a ring at the end of his nose, his nose, his nose,
With a ring at the end of his nose.

"Dear Pig, are you willing to sell for one shilling your ring?"
Said the Piggy, "I will."
So they took it away, and were married next day
By the Turkey who lives on the hill.
They dined on mince, and slices of quince,
Which they ate with a runcible spoon;
And hand in hand, on the edge of the sand,
They danced by the light of the moon, the moon, the moon,
They danced by the light of the moon.

A Lyric from Paul Kelly and The Messengers

I have the moon in my bed
Every night down she falls
I have the moon in my bed
I had nothing, now I have it all
And I have the sun in my heart
When I rise by her side
I have the sun in my heart
Even through the darkest night
She can save me from myself
Make me feel like someone else
When I hardly know myself
I have the moon in my bed
I have the sun in my heart
I have the stars at my feet
I have the moon in my bed

"Love's Philosophy" by Percy Bysshe Shelley

The fountains mingle with the river,
And the rivers with the ocean;
The winds of heaven mix forever,
With a sweet emotion;
Nothing in the world is single;
All things by a law divine
In one another's being mingle; —
Why not I with thine?

See! the mountains kiss high heaven,
And the waves clasp one another;
No sister flower would be forgiven,
If it disdained it's brother;
And the sunlight clasps the earth,
And the moonbeams kiss the sea; —
What are all these kissings worth,
If thou kiss not me?

Sonnet 116 by William Shakespeare

Let me not to the marriage of true minds
Admit impediments. Love is not love
Which alters when it alteration finds,
Or bends with the remover to remove:
O no! it is an ever-fixed mark
That looks on tempests and is never shaken;
It is the star to every wandering bark,
Whose worth's unknown, although his height be taken.
Love's not Time's fool, though rosy lips and cheeks
Within his bending sickle's compass come:
Love alters not with his brief hours and weeks,
But bears it out even to the edge of doom.
If this be error and upon me proved,
I never writ, nor no man ever loved.

Adapted from The Book of Psalms

Blessed are the man and woman, who have grown beyond themselves
And have seen through the illusion of separations
They delight in the way things are
And they keep their hearts open,
Day and night
They are like trees planted near flowing waters
Which bear fruit when they are ready
Their leaves will not wither or die
Everything they do will succeed,
for it is grounded in the Truth.

The Song of Songs 5:1-2

I am come into my garden, my sister, my spouse:
I have gathered my myrrh with my spice;
I have eaten my honeycomb with my honey;
I have drunk my wine with my milk:
Eat, O friends; drink, yea, drink abundantly,
O beloved.
I sleep, but my heart waketh:
It is the voice of my beloved that knocketh, saying, Open to me

From "Leaves of Grass" by Walt Whitman

The day when I arose at dawn from the bed of perfect
health, refresh'd, singing, inhaling the ripe sweet breath of autumn,
When I saw the full moon in the west grow pale and disappear in the morning light,
And when I wander'd alone over the beach, and undressing bathed,
laughing with the cool waters, and saw the sun rise
And when I thought how my dear friend my lover was on
his way coming, O then I was happy,
O then each breath tasted sweeter, and all that day my food
Nourish'd me more, and the beautiful day pass'd well,
And the next came with equal joy, and with the next at evening came my friend,
And that night while all was still I heard the waters roll slowly
continually up the shores,
I heard the hissing rustle of the liquid and sands as directed to me
whispering to congratulate me,
For the one I love most lay sleeping by me under the same cover in the cool night,
In the stillness in the autumn moonbeams his face was inclined toward me,
And his arm lay lightly over my breast — and that night I was happy.

"Had I The Heaven's Embroidered Cloths" by William Butler Yeats

Had I the heaven's embroidered cloths,
Enwrought with golden and silver light,
The blue and the dim and the dark cloths
Of night and light and the half-light,
I would spread the cloths under your feet:
But I, being poor, have only my dreams;
I have spread my dreams under your feet;
Tread softly because you tread on my dreams.

I Pronounce You Husband and Wife

The traditional end of a wedding ceremony is the pronouncement. "I pronounce you husband and wife. You may kiss." I also like to introduce the couple as they will be called in the future. Some brides take their husband's family name. Some brides hyphenate their name, while others retain their birth name.. Here is a prime example that words have power. Everyone recognizes that a name represents one's essence, one's soul; but which comes first, the new identity or the new name? The words which are said during your wedding ceremony are the beginning of a transformation that the pronouncement of your name reflects and amplifies. The ancient derivation of the word *name* means to identify with a mark. Your name is your marker; the wedding ceremony is the energizer which changes your name so that the *I* doesn't disappear, but expands to include the *We*. Words change our perception of the world. The words of your ceremony need to have personal meaning. They need to tell the story which reflects the choice you are making so that the *We* is named on all levels to the depths of your soul. Your ceremony is a naming, a marking, of you as a couple.

In an anti-heroic age, we find it pretentious to think heroically. Yet, that is what a wedding is about, making us into kings and queens with attendants in processional. I am not fond of the stylized Victorian customs that have become the standard for a white wedding, but I do recognize the outsized moment that is a wedding. There are few moments in our lives so full of fear and hope and dreams as our wedding. Use the power of your words to capture that energy, and to connect you to the traditions of the past. Use the power of your words to mark the direction you will take together into the future.

Chapter Eleven

NEW AND
OLD BLESSINGS

What is a vow,
But an intention
Spoken out before the world
So that the world, in hearing,
Might take part
In aspirations
Of the willing heart?
In our coming here today
To join and bless
The joy of your becoming wed,
May we enter in the truth of the words you've said,
"I do."

"INTENTIONALITY" BY MAUREEN TOLMAN FLANNERY

Weddings are a blessing to all involved. A wedding is an affirmation of life, an acknowledgement that our actions create our existence. We say "I do" and instantly self actualize into a new state of being. A wedding states on both a personal and collective level that we are not alone as we pass through the enormity of this universe. Weddings are humanity's consistent denial of alienation, blessings of consistent optimism ultimately expressed in two words: "I do."

I believe weddings need rituals and words of blessing. The nonreligious may be shy of using this term for a ceremony, but a blessing — as derived from Hebrew and Greek usage — means well-spoken words of praise, and does not have to be associated with divinity. In fact, many of the rituals and blessings of contemporary weddings come out of folk tradition and popular culture, rather than religion.

Thus, in recent decades, the TV miniseries "Roots" popularized the African American revival of jumping a broom. As a method of turning humanity into chattel, slaveholders denied marriage to their slaves, but humanity would not be denied. Despite the reality that one might be sold away from partner and children, slaves created their own marriage ritual which ended with the couple jumping over a broomstick. Some say this custom goes back to African fertility rituals which used brooms and straw, but parallel rituals are found in Roman and European corn or grain cultures, and quite possibly the custom comes from the many Irish-Scottish plantation owners whose tradition had the similar folk custom of riding the broom.

Clearly, the ritual carries the intention of blessing the couple with good fortune and fertility. In some traditions, the broomstick becomes a line drawn in the ground, or sticks laid down like the box of a house. The symbolism is the same. Upon marrying, we cross a threshold; but notice, we jump out, not in. The past is left behind, and together we embrace the future. In the last half-century, the popular Apache Wedding blessing has voiced this same thought:

Now you will feel no rain, for each of you is a shelter for the other.
Now you will feel no cold, for each of you is warmth for the other.
Now there is no more loneliness, for each of you will be a companion for the other.
Now you are two persons, but there is only one life before you.
Go now to your dwelling place to begin the days of your life together.
May your days together be good and long upon this earth.

In fact, like so many elements of the modern wedding, the words are not really traditional. They come from a 1950s Hollywood film "Broken Arrow," but they are commonly used because they successfully state the meaning of the moment.

The Irish wedding blessing is another passage that many couples use, even if they are not Irish:

May the road rise to meet you; May the wind be always at your back; May the
sun shine warm upon your face, The rains fall soft upon the fields; May the light
of friendship guide your paths together; May the laughter of children grace the
halls of your home; May the joy of living for one another trip a smile from your
lips, a twinkle from your eye, and when eternity beckons, at the end of a life heaped
high with love, may the good Lord embrace you with the arms that have nurtured
you the whole length of your joy-filled days. May the gracious God hold you both
in the palm of His hands, and, today, may the Spirit of Love find a dwelling place
in your hearts.

A wedding ceremony should acknowledge the universal resonance of the moment as well as the individuals' celebration of their union. A successful wedding ritual should create a silent dialogue between the guests and the officiant — the Amen impulse — which activates a wealth of hope and dreams; and all present now pass these historic and universal wishes or blessings on to the bride and groom.

George Eliot wrote:

What greater thing is there for two human souls than to feel that they are joined for life — to strengthen each other in all labor, to rest on each other in all sorrow, to minister to each other in all pain, to be one with each other in silent unspeakable memories.

Finding the right words to express a contemporary wedding blessing is an exciting cross-cultural exploration. I enjoy when a couple shares a ritual cup of sweet wine. I sometimes use a poem by Robert Herrick as a blessing:

Give me a kiss, and to that kiss a score;
Then to that twenty, add a hundred more:
A thousand to that hundred: so kiss on,
To make that thousand up a million.
Treble that million, and when that is done,
Let's kiss afresh, as when we first begun.

Thus, words and ritual become a formula to make one and one more than two. The *I Ching* can be used to bless the amalgam of a love stronger than its components with these words:

When two people are at one in their inmost hearts,
They shatter even the strength of iron or of bronze;
And when two persons understand each other in their inmost hearts,
Their words are sweet and strong like the fragrance of orchids.

The Jewish mystic, Rabbi Israel, the Baal Shem Tov, expressed the same idea:

From every human being there rises a light that reaches straight to heaven, and when two souls that are designed to be together find each other, their streams of light flow together and a single, brighter light goes forth from their united being.

As does Kuan Tao-Sheng, the Chinese artist and poet:

You and I have so much love,
That it burns like a fire
In which we bake a lump of clay
Molded into a figure of you
And a figure of me.
Then we take both of them,
And break them into pieces with water,
And mold again a figure of you,
And a figure of me.
I am your clay.
You are my clay.
In life we share a single quilt.
In death we will share a single coffin.

And in a simple, but deeply felt statement, Voltaire wrote:

Sensual pleasure passes and vanishes in the twinkling of an eye, but the friendship
between us, the mutual confidence, the delights of the heart, the enchantment
of the soul, these things do not perish and can never be destroyed. I shall love you
until I die.

Often a reading will serve as a blessing. I have been surprised that contemporary couples shy away from classical choices. Don't be intimidated. Great poetry is not hard to read, and English literature offers some of the world's greatest poetry. I have always been charmed by Christopher Marlowe's "Passionate Shepherd to His Love":

Come live with me and be my love,
And we will all the pleasures prove,
That valleys, groves, hills, and fields,
Woods, or steepy mountain yields.

And we will sit upon the rocks,
Seeing the shepherds feed their flocks,
By shallow rivers, to whose falls
Melodious birds sing madrigals.

And I will make thee beds of roses,
And a thousand fragrant posies,
A cap of flowers and a kirtle
Embroider'd all with leaves of myrtle:

A gown made of the finest wool,
Which from our pretty lambs we pull;
Fair lined slippers for the cold,
With buckles of the purest gold:

A belt of straw and ivy buds,
With coral clasps and amber studs;
And if these pleasures may thee move,
Come live with me and be my love.

The shepherd swains shall dance and sing
For thy delight each May morning;
If these delights thy mind may move,
Then live with me and be my love.

Walt Whitman offers a swashbuckling vision of married life:

We will sail pathless and wild seas,
We will go where winds blow, waves dash, and the Yankee
Clipper speeds by under full sail.
Allons! With power, liberty, the earth, the elements,
Health, defiance, gayety, self-esteem, curiosity;
Allons! From all formules!

Camerado, I give you my hand!
I give you my love more precious than money,
I give you myself before preaching or law;
Will you give me yourself? Will you come travel with me?
Shall we stick by each other as long as we live?

Anne Bradstreet, a puritan and one of America's first poets, offers simplicity and sincerity in "To My Dear and Loving Husband":

If ever two were one, then surely we.
If ever man were lov'd by wife, then thee;
If ever wife was happy in a man,
Compare with me ye women if you can.
I prize thy love more than whole Mines of gold,
Or all the riches that the East doth hold.
My love is such that Rivers cannot quench,
Nor ought but love from thee, give recompense.
Thy love is such I can no way repay;
The heavens reward thee manifold I pray.
Then while we live, in love let's so persevere,
That when we live no more, we may live ever.

Although modern, The Australian poet Christopher Brennan strikes a classical vein with his poem "Because She Would Ask Me Why I Loved Her":

If questioning would make us wise
No eyes would ever gaze in eyes;
If all our tale were told in speech
No mouths would wander each to each.

Were spirits free from mortal mesh
And love not bound in hearts of flesh
No aching breasts would yearn to meet
And find their ecstasy complete.

For who is there that lives and knows
The secret powers by which he grows?
Were knowledge all, what were our need
To thrill and faint and sweetly bleed?

Then seek not, sweet, the "If" and "Why"
I love you now until I die.
For I must love because I live
And life in me is what you give.

Much of the power of a blessing comes from its placement in the ceremony. Unfortunately, many guests arrive at a wedding expecting to endure the ceremony and to enjoy the party. When I began to officiate at weddings, I was shocked that cell phones commonly interrupt. Obviously, the guests did not sense that they were coming into a special space where a significant experience awaits. When I began to routinely request a "Turn Off Your Cell Phones" announcement, many couples feared it would sound tacky. However, as I continued to battle ring tones during ceremonies, I began to insist, and I discovered that adversity is a blessing. While everyone waited for the phones to power down, I could read a short poem which blessed the space for the purpose of celebrating the love that had brought us together that night. My words focused the guests, and the heightened language changed the space from the profane banquet hall into a sacred place of celebration. My favorite author for this moment is Jose Marti:

Love is born
With the pleasure of looking at each other.
It is fed
With the necessity of seeing each other.
It is concluded with the impossibility
Of ever being apart.

A couple who had a beach wedding chose a poem "Beach Chairs" by Joyce Ebrecht:

Sitting on the beach chairs
watching the setting sun,
holding hands and reminiscing
how it all began.

Sitting on the beach chairs
watching the ships out on the sea,
holding hands and smiling
together we're meant to be.

Sitting on the beach chairs
watching people walking past,
holding hands and knowing
that our love will always last.

Sitting on the beach chairs
watching the waves along the shore,
holding hands we realize
our love is stronger than before.

Sitting on the beach chairs
watching the changing tide,
holding hands with happiness
to be by each other's side.

Sitting on the beach chairs
watching the sunrise,
holding hands with tears of joy
there are no more good-byes.

Beginnings also give the opportunity to state the story being told. A public ceremony is both a witnessing and a wishing. We bless this couple with the hopes expressed in this anonymous poem:

If you can love each
Through the sunshine and the storm,
And keep the flame of true devotion
Glowing bright and warm;

If you can give each other room
To grow and change and learn,
Yet still hold one another close
In mutual concern;

If you can be both lovers,
And the very best of friends,
And face together, hand in hand,
The challenges life sends;

If you can offer patience, comfort
And real understanding,
Encourage one another's efforts
Yet be undemanding;

If you can show true love and faith
In everything you do,
Then married life will surely hold
Much joy for both of you.

Or using the words of Dante Alighieri from "La Vita Nuova," we see the moment as mystery, two lives trusting in each other to write a story not yet told:

In that book which is
My memory...
On the first page
That is the chapter when
I first met you
Appear the words...
Here begins a new life

Often, my wedding couples ask for readings and blessings from traditional American religions. The concept of a Civil Celebrant is inclusive. Even if you desire a secular wedding, do not ignore the power of readings from scripture or from the wisdom of the three Abrahamic traditions. These words resonate within our cultural history. They are valid and beautiful. Ecclesiastes 4 9:12 says:

Two are better than one, because they have a good return for their work; if one
falls down, his friend can help him up. But pity the man who falls and has no
one to help him up! Also, if two lie down together, they will keep warm. But how
can one keep warm alone? Though one may be over powered, two can defend
themselves. A cord of three strands is not quickly broken.

The Jewish seven wedding blessings are easily adapted to a joyous offering of spirituality and community and a wonderful setting at the end of the ceremony for the traditional breaking of a wine glass:

Blessed are we for the gift of the fruit of the vine, symbol of Joy.
Blessed are we to be part of the glory of the Universe.
Blessed are we to be born human.
Blessed are we to have been born male and female and for the joy and fruit
of that division.
Blessed are we by the union of our children. Blessed are we that these companions
in friendship and love rejoice as bride and bridegroom.
Blessed are we for the gifts of joy and gladness, bride and bridegroom, mirth and
exultation, pleasure and delight, love, brotherhood, peace and fellowship. Soon
there will be heard in the halls and on the streets, the voices of the bride and the
bridegroom, the jubilant voices of those joined in marriage and of the young
and old feasting and singing. Blessed are we to see the joy of the bride and the
joy of the groom.

The traditional wedding prayer of St. Francis of Assisi is a moving blessing. I have used it in conjunction with a tradition I saw at a Quaker wedding. As part of the vow taking, elders and/or members of the wedding party ask the couple a series of questions:

Will you love each other?
Yes

Will you hurt each other?
Yes

Will you support each other?
Yes

Will you fail each other intentionally or unintentionally?
Yes

Will you forgive each other?
Yes

Will you persevere with each other come what may?
Yes

Will you strive to be the best life partner and friend you can be?
Yes

Will you disappoint each other?
Yes

Will you strive to change what is hurtful and encourage
all that makes you prosper as husband and wife?
Yes

OFFICIANT:
Please repeat after me —

Where there is hatred, let us sow love
Where there is injury, let us bring the spirit of forgiveness
Where there is discord, let us bring harmony
Where there is doubt, let us bring faith
Where there is despair, let us bring hope
Where there is darkness, let us bring light
Where there is sadness, let us bring joy
For it is in giving that we receive
It is in forgiving that we are forgiven

I have used Biblical text in several bilingual weddings. The translations are accessible and the poetry is among the world's greatest. I recommend Colossians 3:12-14:

> Put on then, to your beloved, compassion, kindness, lowliness, meekness, and patience, forbearing one another and, if one has a complaint against another, forgiving each other; so you also must be forgiven. And above all these put on love, which binds everything together in perfect harmony.

And, although the text tends toward the theatrical if not placed in the right context, I am particularly partial to the "Song of Solomon" which is among the world's greatest love poetry.

2:10-13

My lover spoke and said to me,
"Arise, my darling,
my beautiful one, and come with me.
See! The winter is past;
the rains are over and gone.
Flowers appear on the earth;
the season of singing has come,
the cooing of doves
is heard in our land.
The fig tree forms its early fruit;
the blossoming vines spread their fragrance.
Arise, come, my darling;
my beautiful one, come with me."

— OR —

8:6-7

Place me like a seal over your heart,
like a seal on your arm;
for love is as strong as death,
its jealousy unyielding as the grave.
It burns like blazing fire,
like a mighty flame.
Many waters cannot quench love;
rivers cannot wash it away.
If one were to give
all the wealth of his house for love,
it would be utterly scorned.

Probably the most popular Biblical quote for American weddings is from 1 Corinthians 13. I use this adaptation:

Love is always patient and kind; It is never jealous;
Love is neither boastful or conceited;
It is never rude or selfish; It does not take offense; It is not resentful.
Love takes no pleasure in other people's faults, but delights in the truth;
It is always ready to excuse, to trust, to hope. It is always ready to
endure whatever comes. Finally, true love does not come to an end.
Now these three remain: Faith, Hope, and Love, but the greatest of these is Love.

A particularly moving story and quote comes from the Story of Ruth 1: 16-17.

Where you go, and where you stay I will stay. Your people will be my people
and your God, my God. Where you die, I will die, and there I will be buried.
May the Lord deal with me, be it ever so severely, if anything but death
separates you and me.

Many blessings come from folk or philosophical teachings. I find this Muslim quote appealing:

The doors of Heaven to mercy will be opened in four situations: when it rains,
when a child looks kindly at his parent's face, when the Ka'bah is opened,
and when marriage occurs.

This old English blessing is charming:

May your joys be as bright as the morning, your vows of happiness as numerous
as the stars in the heavens, and your troubles but shadows that fade in the
sunlight of love.

And this Hindu poem reminds me of the rich colors and sensuality of the miniature paintings I saw in the palaces of Rajasthan:

You have become mine forever.
Yes, we have become partners.
I have become yours.
Hereafter, I cannot live without you.
Do not live without me.
Let us share the joys.
We are word and meaning, united.
You are thought and I am sound.

May the nights be honey-sweet for us.
May the mornings be honey-sweet for us.
May the plants be honey-sweet for us.
May the earth be honey-sweet for us.

Of course, Kahil Gibran remains popular and often quoted:

Love one another,
But make not a bond of love.
Let it rather be a moving sea
Between the shores of your souls.

Fill each other's cup
But drink not from the same cup.
Sing and dance together and be joyous,
But let each one of you be alone
Though they quiver with the same music.

Give your hearts,
But not into the other's keeping,
For only the hand of life
Can contain your hearts.

And stand together
Yet not too near together;
For the pillars of the temple stand apart,
And the oak tree and the cypress
Grow not in each other's shadows.

The very popular advice from Wilfred Peterson's "The Art of Marriage" is alleged to be one of the most frequently quoted passages at American weddings:

A good marriage must be created.
In the Art of marriage the little things are the big things —
It is never being too old to hold hands.
It is remembering to say 'I Love You' at least once each day.
It is never going to sleep angry.
It is having a mutual sense of values and common objectives.
It is standing together facing the world.
It is forming a circle of love that gathers in the whole family.
It is speaking words of appreciation and demonstrating gratitude in thoughtful ways.
It is having the capacity to forgive and forget.
It is giving each other an atmosphere in which each can grow.
It is finding room for the things of the spirit.
It is a common search for the good and the beautiful.
It is not only marrying the right partner —
It is being the right partner.

In this Internet age, many more quotes can be found at wedding websites. In this chapter, I have compiled some of my favorites. There are three readings that I use over and over again. You will see them in many of the ceremonies I include in this book. They are simple and heartfelt, and they are my wish for all the many lives I have touched.

Mark Twain wrote:

A marriage makes of two fractional lives a whole,
Gives to two purposeless lives a work,
And doubles the strength of each to perform it;
It gives it two questioning natures
A reason for living and something to live for;
It will give a new gladness to the sunshine,
A new fragrance to the flowers,
A new beauty to the earth,
and a new mystery to life.

I always feel like I am summoning the universe when I say these words:

May you and your love be blessed from all directions.
From the sacred east — where the flaming sun arises
Let your love be a light and inspiration to yourselves and to the world.
May all your mornings be blessed with love.
The sacred south- where the earth offers her abundance
Let your love support our planting and harvesting,
both as individuals and as a couple.
May all your days be blessed with love.
The sacred west- where the noble sun sets
Let your love be a comfort to all your disappointments,
a mirror to all your hopes,
May all your nights be blessed with love.
The sacred north- where the soul's compass finds its home
Let your love be a guide to your passion and powers and your progress
in the world
May all your years be blessed with love.

These are the sacred directions of love —
May you be held within their center — Now and for the rest of your life
together and may all your dreams come true.

No more need be said than this wish for a new couple:

May all that you are, always be in love.
May all that is love, always be in you.
May your love be as beautiful on each day you share,
as it is on this day of celebration; and may each day you share
be as precious to you as the day you first fell in love.
May you always see and encourage the best in each other.
May the challenges life brings your way make your marriage even stronger,
And may you always be each other's best friend and greatest love.

So may we all be blessed!

Chapter Twelve

LEGALLY
EVER AFTER

Getting your marriage license is your responsibility. The legislature of each state makes its respective marriage laws, but a town or county clerk issues you the license, and sometimes will have his or her own rules and procedures. I suggest you check well in advance, paying special attention to the clerk's office hours.

Every state has different requirements, and every clerk handles the paperwork differently. The New York City Clerk's office is wonderfully efficient. On the other hand, I have had the occasion of a small-town clerk mislaying the paperwork. When the license had not arrived in the mail, the bride called to inquire. Much to her panic, she was told the clerk had no record of the marriage. (That is why I always make a copy before I mail the license in to the appropriate clerk.) A few calming phone calls later, the license was found...misfiled. Stuff happens. Nothing is irreparable if you are dealing with a responsible wedding officiant, but I do suggest you stay on top of the process.

Most states will issue a license within the month preceding the ceremony. Some require waiting periods after the license is issued. In general, you no longer need a blood test. All the states recognize each other's marriage laws with the exception of same-sex marriages, exempted from reciprocity by the federal Defense of Marriage Act. You will need a specifically defined ID, and you may have to bring a witness with you to obtain your license. Sometimes you need to make an appointment. If you are under 18, you will need to bring your parents or a legal guardian. In this case, I suggest you wait until you are legally competent. In general, it is good to have cash to pay the fees, as many clerks do not accept charge cards or personal checks.

Every state and every clerk is different. You must get your license in the state where you are getting married. Check the Internet for the state rules and make a phone call to the appropriate clerk before you go to get your license. Weddings make people happy. In general, everyone will be delighted to answer your questions.

In this chapter, I have compiled the basic rules for each state and the District of Columbia as of 2010, but rules change, as do fees. I am not a lawyer, and this chapter is not legal advice.

Alabama

You will need your birth certificate or driver's license and your Social Security number. If you were divorced within the last six months, you will need a copy of your divorce decree. In all cases, I advise that you know the beginning and ending dates of any previous marriage and the location of the decree. If a marriage has ended with the death of a spouse, you will need to know the date of death. You cannot get married within 60 days after a divorce. Otherwise, you can get married immediately after issuance of a license, which is good for 30 days. You can marry your first cousin, but you cannot marry someone of the same sex. Wedding officiants must be ministers of recognized religious organizations or current or retired Alabama judges. Your licensing fee is $43.35.

Alaska

You will need a picture ID. You can fax or mail your application into the clerk, in which case, your application must be notarized. If you were divorced within the last 60 days, you will need a copy of your divorce decree. Know the beginning and ending dates of any previous marriage and the location of the decree. You will need a copy of the divorce decree if divorced within 60 days of your new marriage. You must wait at least three days after the clerk receives your application to use your license. The license is only valid for 30 days. You can marry your first cousin, but you cannot marry someone of the same sex. Wedding officiants must be a minister, priest, recognized leader, or rabbi of any church or congregation in the state, a commissioned officer of the Salvation Army, marriage commissioner, or a judicial officer of the state. Your licensing fee is $25.

Arizona

You will need a driver's license or birth certificate for proof of age. (Some counties require a birth certificate if you are less than 30 years of age). You will not need a copy of your divorce decree. Know the beginning and ending dates of any previous marriage and the location of the decree. The license is valid for one year. You can marry your first cousin if you are both over 65 or if one of you is over 65 and can show that you are not able to bear children; but you cannot marry someone of the same sex. Wedding officiants must be a member of the clergy, a judge, a magistrate, a clerk of the circuit court, or a clerk or clerk-treasurer of a city or town. Your licensing fee is $72.

Arkansas

If you are not yet 21 years of age, you will need a certified copy of your birth certificate, a passport, or an active military ID card. If you are over 21 years of age, you will need a valid driver's license. You will need a copy of your divorce decree. Know the beginning and ending dates of any previous marriage and the location of the decree. The license is only valid for 60 days and must be returned to the clerk if unused. You cannot marry your first cousin, nor can you marry someone of the same sex. Wedding officiants must have their credentials recorded in one of Arkansas's 75 counties. Your licensing fee varies from county to county, but will range from $35-$47.

California

You will need a picture ID such as a driver's license or passport. Some counties recommend bringing a certified copy of your birth certificate. You will need to know your parents' names and where they were born. The rules vary from county to county, but if you divorced within the past year, you will need a copy of your divorce decree. In cases of death or annulment of a previous marriage, you must also bring proof. The license is valid for 90 days. You can marry your first cousin; the issue of same-sex marriage is being legally challenged in the courts. It was yes, then no, with some couples having been legally married. Wedding officiants can be clergy, judges, magistrates, marriage commissioners (current or retired) and, in some counties, family and friends who register. Your fee will be $45 or more depending on the county.

Colorado

You will need a driver's license, passport, or military ID, as well as your Social Security card. If you were previously married, you will need a copy of the divorce decree or your spouse's death certificate. There is no waiting period, and your license is valid for 30 days. You can marry your first cousin, but not a partner of the same sex. Couples may register to solemnize their own marriage or have a judge, retired judge, magistrate, clergy or authorized public official perform the ceremony. Your fee will be $10 and up, depending on the county.

Connecticut

You will need a photo ID such as a driver's license or passport, as well as your Social Security numbers, your parents' names, mother's maiden name and your parents' places of birth, date and location of your wedding, and the name and contact information of your wedding officiant. You need to apply in your town of residence or in the town where the ceremony will take place. You will need a copy of your divorce decree or have the date, county and state of death of a previous spouse. If your name has changed, you need to bring a certified copy of your divorce decree. There is no waiting period, but often the clerk will not have the finished paperwork to give to you until the next day. The license is valid for 65 days. You can marry your cousin, and Connecticut recognizes marriages of same-sex couples. Wedding officiants must be a judge, retired judge, Connecticut state referee, Connecticut justices of the peace, or an ordained or licensed clergyman. Your fee will be approximately $35, varying slightly town to town.

Delaware

You will need a photo ID such as a driver's license or passport. You will need a certified copy of your divorce decree or the death certificate of a deceased spouse. There is a 24-hour waiting period for residents and a 96-hour waiting period if you are both non-residents. The license is valid for 30 days. You cannot marry your first cousin or a partner of the same sex. Wedding officiants must be clergy or clerks of the peace. Your fee will be $35.

Florida

You must have a picture ID such as a driver's license, your Social Security card, or a valid passport or an I-94 card. You may be asked for a certified copy of your birth certificate. You will need a certified copy of your divorce decree if you were divorced within the last 30 days, or a death certificate if your former spouse has died within that same time period. If the period has been longer than 30 days, you need only the date of the decree or death. There is a three-day waiting period. Your license is valid for 60 days. You may marry your first cousin, but not a partner of the same sex. Wedding officiants must be ordained or licensed clergy, justices of the peace, or notary publics. Your fee will be $93.50.

Georgia

You must have two valid IDs such as driver's license, passport, birth certificate, or military ID, and, if divorced, a copy of your final divorce decree. You will have to fill out a form. If you are a nonresident of Georgia, you must obtain your license in the county in which the ceremony will take place. There is no waiting period, and the license does not have a predetermined expiration period. You may marry your first cousin, but not a partner of the same sex. Officiants must be licensed or ordained ministers of recognized religious societies or justices of the peace. Your license will cost $65 except if you have taken a state-certified premarital counseling course. In this case, the fee will be $30.

Hawaii

If you are 18 years of age, you must show a birth certificate. If you are 19 years or older, a valid driver's license is sufficient for proof of age. If you were formerly married, you must state the date of the final divorce decree or, if your spouse is deceased, the date of death. There is no waiting period, and the license does not have a predetermined expiration date. You may marry your first cousin, but not a partner of the same sex. Officiants must be commissioned by the State of Hawaii, Department of Health. Your license will cost $60.

Idaho

You must have a birth certificate and driver's license and your Social Security number. If you have been previously married, you must have the date of your divorce decree or the date of your spouse's death. You need to read and sign a premarital AIDS education pamphlet. You cannot marry your first cousin, or a partner of the same sex. There is no waiting period and your license has no expiration date. Your officiant must be a minister, priest, judge, or designated government official. Your fee will be $28 on weekdays and $45 dollars on Saturdays.

Illinois

You must have proof of age and identity such as a driver's license, state or military ID, or passport, or any two of the following: certified birth certificate or baptismal certificate, a life insurance policy in effect for at least one year, U.S. Alien resident card, foreign passport, or naturalization papers. If you are divorced within the last six months, you must bring a certified copy of your divorce decree. There is a 24-hour waiting period, and your license is good for 60 days within the county where it was issued. You may marry your first cousin if you are over 50 years of age, but you cannot marry a partner of the same sex. Your officiant must be an ordained minister, priest, current or retired judge, or government official designated to solemnize marriages. Your fee will be $30.

Indiana

You must have proof of age and current address such as a driver's license or ID. If you are less than 30 years old, you may need a certified birth certificate. If previously married, you must know the month and year when your previous marriage ended. A certified divorce decree is recommended. Indiana residents must apply in their county of residence. There is no waiting period, and your license is good for 60 days. You may marry your first cousin if you are both over 65 years of age, but you cannot marry a partner of the same sex. Your officiant must be a member of the clergy, a judge, a magistrate, a clerk of the circuit court, or a clerk or clerk-treasurer of a city or town. Your fee will be $18 if you are a resident or $60 for nonresidents.

Iowa

You must have photo ID and Social Security number. You must have a witness with you when you file for your license. If previously married, you will need the date of your divorce decree or the date of your spouse's death. If you have been divorced within the last 60 days, you will need a signed copy of the divorce decree. There is a three-day waiting period, and the license is good for six months. You cannot marry your first cousin, but you can marry a partner of the same sex. Your fee will be $30.

Kansas

You will need photo ID such as a driver's license and your Social Security card. If previously married, you will need the date of the final divorce decree or the date of your spouse's death. In some counties, you may have to wait 30 days after a divorce before you can remarry. There is a three-day waiting period, and your license is valid for six months. You cannot marry your first cousin, nor can you marry a partner of the same sex. Your officiant must be an ordained minister or a judge of a court. Your fee will be $75. ($50 plus a $25 surcharge)

Kentucky

You will need a photo ID such as a driver's license. Your Social Security card and/or birth certificate may be helpful. If you have been previously married, you will need a copy of the divorce decree or death certificate. There is no waiting period, and your license is valid for 30 days. You cannot marry your first cousin, nor can you marry a partner of the same sex. Your officiant must be a minister who is licensed in Kentucky to perform weddings, or a justice of the peace. Your fee will be $36 or slightly less, depending on the county.

Louisiana

You must have a photo ID such as a driver's license, and a certified copy of your birth certificate. You will also need your Social Security number, your parents' full name, mother's maiden name, and the state in which you were born. If you were previously married, you will need a certified copy of the divorce decree or the death certificate. There is a 72-hour waiting period with an exception for out of state residents being married in New Orleans. The license is valid for 30 days. You cannot marry your first cousin, nor can you marry a partner of the same sex. Your officiant must be an ordained minister who has registered with the clerk of the district court of the parish, or the New Orleans Department of Health, or a justice of the peace. Your fee will be approximately $25 with fees varying from parish to parish.

Maine

You will only need a driver's license if you are 24 years of age or older. Otherwise, you will need your birth certificate or a passport. You will also need your Social Security number. Residents need to apply in one of their home towns. If previously married, you will need a certified copy of the divorce decree or death certificate. There is no waiting period, and your license is valid for 90 days. You can marry your first cousin, and you can marry a partner of the same sex. Your officiant must be an ordained minister licensed by the secretary of state, a notary public, or a member of the Maine Bar. Your fee will be $30.

Maryland

You will need a driver's license or birth certificate. You must be married in the county in which you purchase your license. If you were previously married, you will need your divorce decree or have information regarding date, county and state of death of your previous spouse. There is a waiting period of 48 hours, and your license is valid for six months. You can marry your first cousin, but you cannot marry a partner of the same sex. Your officiant must be an official of a religious order, a deputy clerk, or a judge. Your fee will be $35-$60 depending on the county.

Massachusetts

You will need proper ID; a certified birth certificate is suggested. Some counties may require you to wait 90 days before remarrying. There is a three-day waiting period, unless one partner is close to death or about to give birth. In which case, a request by a clergyman or doctor to waive the waiting period will be honored. Your license is valid for 60 days. You can marry your first cousin, and you can marry a partner of the same sex. Your officiant must be a member of the clergy or a justice of the peace. Out-of-state clergy must obtain a certificate of authorization from the Massachusetts Secretary of the Commonwealth. A non-minister or non-justice of the peace can obtain a onetime special permission to perform a marriage by paying the governor's office a $25 fee. Your fee will be $4-$50 depending on the township.

Michigan

You will need a photo ID such as a driver's license or a military ID, plus a certified copy of your birth certificate. Foreign birth certificates must be translated into English and notarized. You will need your parents' address and your mother's maiden name. If you were previously married, you will most likely need a copy of the divorce decree or death certificate. You may have to leave the documents with the clerk. Residents need to apply in their home county while nonresidents need to apply in the county where they will marry. There is a three-day waiting period, and the license is valid for 30 days. Your officiant must be a federal, probate, district, or municipal judge, or a district court magistrate, in their court area; mayors, in their city; county clerks; ministers and pastors of the gospel, both resident and nonresident, or a couple can solemnize their marriage "in the manner heretofore used and practiced in their respective societies or denominations." You cannot marry your first cousin, nor can you marry a partner of the same sex. Your fee will be $20 if a resident or $30 if a nonresident.

Minnesota

You will need proper ID and your Social Security number. If you have been previously married, you must show proof of divorce, annulment, or death. There is a five-day waiting period, and your license is valid for six months. You cannot marry your first cousin, nor can you marry a partner of the same sex. Your officiant must be a judge, clerk of court, court commissioner, or licensed minister, priest or rabbi, or a representative of Bahai, Hindu, Quaker or an American Indian religious group. Your fee will be $40 if you take the state-offered premarital education course or $110 if you do not.

Mississippi

You will need a photo ID such as a driver's license or military ID. Your Social Security card or birth certificate will be helpful. You will need to know your parents' address and your mother's maiden name. If you were previously married, you need to sign an affidavit stating the date and manner by which your last marriage ended. If you were divorced within the last six months, some counties may ask for a copy of the divorce decree. There is a 72-hour waiting period, and your license is good indefinitely. You will need a blood test drawn within the 30 days before you apply which certifies that you are free of syphilis. You cannot marry your first cousin, nor can you marry a partner of the same sex. Your officiant must be a member of the clergy, a mayor, a local board of supervisors member, or a judge of the state of Mississippi supreme court, court of appeals, circuit court, chancery court, justice court, or county court. Your fee will be $22.

Missouri

You must go to the Recorder of Deeds office. You will need ID and your Social Security number. Requirements may vary, as each county in Missouri could have its own requirements. If you were previously married, you will have to show the date your last marriage ended. You will have to wait 30 days after a final divorce decree before you can remarry. There is no waiting period, and your license is valid for 30 days. You cannot marry your first cousin nor can you marry a partner of the same sex. Your officiant must be an ordained minister, active or retired, who is in good standing with his or her congregation; a circuit court or associate circuit court judge who can't receive compensation for performing a marriage ceremony; a marriage commissioner, or an active or retired judge of the Missouri circuit or district court. Your fee will be approximately $60, depending on the county.

Montana

You will need driver's license or a certified birth certificate, plus your Social Security number. If you were previously married, you will need a certified copy of the divorce decree. The bride is required to take a blood test for rubella unless she is over 50 years of age. There is no waiting period, and your license is valid for 180 days. You cannot marry your first cousin, nor can you marry your partner of the same sex. Your officiant must be an ordained or licensed minister, a mayor, a city judge, a tribal judge, or a justice of the peace. Your fee will be $58.

Nebraska

You will need a photo ID such as a driver's license or passport, as well as your Social Security numbers. You will need to know your parents' names as well as your mother's maiden name and your parents' birthplaces. If you have been previously married, you will need to provide the date of your final divorce decree or the date of death. In some counties, you cannot marry for six months after a divorce. There is no waiting period, and your license is valid for one year. You cannot marry your first cousin, nor can you marry a partner of the same sex. Your officiant must be an ordained minister, an active or retired judge, or a clerk magistrate. Officiants do not have to reside in Nebraska. Your fee will be $15.

Nevada

You will need a photo ID such as a driver's license, passport, military ID, or certified birth certificate. A foreign birth certificate must be translated into English and notarized. If you were previously married, you will need to know the date of your final divorce decree. There is no waiting period, and your license is valid for one year. You cannot marry your first cousin, nor can you marry a partner of the same sex. Your officiant must be an ordained or licensed clergyman who has obtained a certificate of permissions to perform marriages, or a justice of the peace. Your fee will vary from $35-$65.

New Hampshire

You will need photo ID such as your driver's license. If you are 25 years of age or younger, you may need to show a certified birth certificate. You will need your Social Security number. If you have been previously married, you will need a certified copy of your divorce decree or your deceased spouse's death certificate. There is no waiting period, and your license is valid for 90 days. You cannot marry your first cousin, but you may have a civil union with a partner of the same sex. Your officiant must be a judge, supreme court justice, assistant judge, justice of the peace, priest, rabbi, or minister residing in New Hampshire. Nonresident clergy can obtain a special license from the secretary of state. Your fee will be $45.

New Jersey

You must apply in the bride's town of residence, or if the bride is not a New Jersey resident, you must apply in the groom's town of residence. If neither is a New Jersey resident, you must apply in the town where the ceremony will be taking place. You will need to show a photo ID, as well as proof of residency with a driver's license, a tax bill, a utility bill, or an apartment lease plus a certified birth certificate, a passport, an alien card or naturalization papers. You will need your Social Security numbers. Military personnel are considered residents at the base where they are stationed. You will need a witness when you apply for your license. If you have been previously married, you will need a certified copy of your divorce decree or your deceased spouse's death certificate. There is a three-day waiting period, and your license is valid for 30 days. You can marry your first cousin, and you may have a civil union with a partner of the same sex. Your officiant must be a judge of a federal district court, U. S. magistrate, judge of a municipal court, superior court, or tax court, retired judge of the superior court, or judge of the superior or tax court who has resigned in good standing, any mayor/deputy mayor, or chairman of any township committee, a village president of New Jersey, county clerk, and any minister of any religion. At the time you apply for your marriage license you will have to provide the name of who will marry you, where, and when, and an address and phone number for the officiant. Your fee will be $28.

New Mexico

You will need a driver's license, or a passport, or birth certificate, as well as your Social Security number. If you were previously married, you will need to know the date of your divorce decree or the date of your deceased spouse's death. There is no waiting period, and your license is valid for one year. You may marry your first cousin, but you cannot marry a partner of the same sex. Your officiant must be an ordained or licensed clergy or a justice of the peace. Your fee will be $25-$40.

New York

You will need a photo ID such as a current driver's license or passport, and, often, a certified birth certificate. If you have been previously married, you will need a certified copy of your divorce decree or your deceased spouse's death certificate. There is a 24-hour waiting period, and your license is good for 60 days. You may marry your first cousin, but you cannot marry a partner of the same sex. New York does recognize same-sex marriages from other states. Your officiant must be an authorized, officially ordained member of the clergy, or a public official in the State of New York such as a mayor, city clerk, deputy city clerk, appointed marriage officer, justice, or judge. In New York City, an officiant must be registered with the City of New York. Your fee will vary from $35-$50, depending on the locality. Many clerks will only accept money orders.

North Carolina

You will need proof of age such as a driver's license, certified birth certificate, passport, or military ID. You will need to show proof of your Social Security number. If you have been previously married, you must know the date of the divorce decree or your spouse's death. If you were divorced within the last 60 days, you will need a copy of the decree. There is no waiting period, and your license is good for 60 days. You can marry your first cousin, but you cannot marry a partner of the same sex. Your officiant needs to be ordained clergy or a magistrate. Your fee will be $50.

North Dakota

You will need a driver's license or certified birth certificate and your Social Security card. If you were previously married, you will need a certified copy of your divorce decree or a copy of your deceased spouse's death certificate. There is no waiting period, and your license is valid for 60 days. You cannot marry your first cousin, nor can you marry a partner of the same sex. Your officiant must be ordained clergy or a justice of the peace. Your fee will be $65.

Ohio

You will need a government-issued ID such as a driver's license, a passport or visa, or a state ID. You will need to know your Social Security number. If you were previously married, you will need a certified copy of your divorce decree or a copy of your deceased spouse's death certificate. There is no waiting period, and your license is valid for 60 days. You cannot marry your first cousin, nor can you marry a partner of the same sex. Your officiant must be any clergyman who has presented ordination credentials to the county probate judge, or a justice of the peace. Your fee will be approximately $50, depending on the county.

Oklahoma

You will need a driver's license or a certified birth certificate or a passport, as well as your Social Security number. If you were previously married, you will need a copy of the divorce decree. You cannot get married within six months of being divorced. If your former spouse is deceased, know the date of death. There is no waiting period, and your license is valid for 10 days. You cannot marry your first cousin, nor can you marry a partner of the same sex. Your officiant must be ordained clergy who has registered with the county clerk where the ceremony will take place, or a justice of the peace or judge. Your fee will vary from $25-$50. Couples who take premarital counseling from an approved health or religious professional will only be charged $5 for their license.

Oregon

You will need a driver's license or ID card. If you were previously married, you will need to know the date of the divorce decree. Some counties may require a copy of the final divorce decree. You can be married one day after your divorce is final. There is a three-day waiting period, and your license is valid for 60 days. You cannot marry your first cousin, nor can you marry a partner of the same sex, but you register as domestic partners. Your officiant must be a judge, a county clerk or their deputy, a justice of the peace, or ordained clergy. Your fee will vary from $50-$60.

Pennsylvania

You will need photo ID such as a driver's license, passport, or state ID, and your Social Security number. Foreign documents must be translated, and if you cannot speak English, you must be accompanied by a translator. If you were previously married, you will need a certified copy of the final divorce decree or know the date of your deceased spouse's death. There is a three-day waiting period, and your license is valid for 60 days. You cannot marry your first cousin, nor can you marry a partner of the same sex. Your officiant must be an ordained minister, priest or rabbi of any regularly established church or congregation, a mayor, a judge, a justice of the peace, a county clerk or their appointed deputies. Pennsylvania also has the Quaker tradition of a self-uniting marriage. Check with the county clerk to obtain permission. Your fee will vary from $40-$75.

Rhode Island

You will need your birth certificate and your Social Security number. If you were previously married, you will need your divorce decree or the death certificate of your deceased spouse. There is no waiting period, and your license is valid for 90 days. You can marry your first cousin, but you cannot marry a partner of the same sex. Your officiant must be an ordained clergy member of any denomination, or a judge, active or retired, of any court. Your fee will be $24.

South Carolina

You will need proof of ID such as your driver's license or birth certificate or passport, and your Social Security card. You do not need proof of divorce, but know the date of the divorce decree or your spouse's death. Some counties have a 24-hour waiting period. You must check with the clerk. Your license has no expiration period. You can marry your first cousin, but you cannot marry a partner of the same sex. Your officiant must be an ordained member of the clergy or a justice of the peace. Your fee will be $25 and up, depending on the county.

South Dakota

You will need a driver's license or a certified copy of your birth certificate. If you were previously married, you will need a certified copy of your divorce decree or a copy of your deceased spouse's death certificate. There is no waiting period, and your license is valid for 20 days. You cannot marry your first cousin, nor can you marry a partner of the same sex. Your officiant must be an ordained minister, a justice of the supreme court, judge of the circuit court, magistrate, or justice of the peace. Your fee will be $45.

Tennessee

You will need a driver's license or certified birth certificate or passport. You will need to have proof of your Social Security number. If you were previously married, you will need to have a copy of your divorce decree. There is no waiting period, and your license is valid for 30 days. You can marry your first cousin, but you cannot marry a partner of the same sex. Your officiant must be an ordained or licensed clergyman over the age of 18, or justice of the peace, a member of county legislative bodies, a county executive or former county executives, a current or former judge and chancellor of the state, current and former judges of general sessions courts, current and former governors of the state, the county clerk of each county, the current and former speakers of the senate and speakers of the house of representatives, and the mayors of municipalities. Your fee will be $93.50-$99.50 with a $60 discount if you have taken a premarital-preparation course.

Texas

You will need proof of ID such as a driver's license, a passport, a certified birth certificate, a U.S. passport or military card, and your Social Security number. If you were previously married, you must wait 30 days before remarrying or show a divorce decree waiving the 30-day waiting period. There is a 72-hour waiting period after you have applied for your license, and your license is valid for 30 days. You cannot marry your first cousin, nor can you marry a partner of the same sex. Your officiant must be a licensed or ordained Christian minister, priest, Jewish rabbi, officer authorized by religious organizations, justice of the supreme court, judge of the court of criminal appeals, justice of the court of appeals, judge of the district, county, and probate courts, judge of the county courts at law, judge of the courts of domestic relations, judge of the juvenile courts, retired justices or judge, justice of the peace, retired justice of the peace, or a judge or magistrate of a federal court of Texas. Your fee will vary from $31-$41. The fee will be waived if you take an eight-hour premarital-preparation course.

Utah

You will need a driver's license, passport, birth certificate, and your Social Security number. You need to know your parents' names and birthplaces and your mother's maiden name. If you were previously married, you need to know the date of your divorce decree or the date of your deceased spouse's death. There is no waiting period, and your license is valid for 30 days. You can marry your first cousin if you are over 65 years of age or can prove that you are incapable of reproduction. You cannot marry a partner of the same sex. Your officiant must be an ordained minister who is at least 18 years of age, a Native American spiritual advisor, the governor, a mayor, justice of the peace, judge or commissioner, county clerk, president of the senate, speaker of the House of Representatives, retired judge or magistrate, or a U.S. judge or magistrate. Your fee will be $45-$50 depending on the county.

Vermont

You will need a driver's license or a certified birth certificate. You will need to know your parents' names, your mother's maiden name, and their birthplaces. If you were previously married, you will need a certified copy of your divorce decree or a copy of your deceased spouse's death certificate. There is no waiting period, and your license is valid for 60 days. You can marry your first cousin as long as you come from a state that allows cousin marriage, and you can marry a partner of the same sex. Your officiant must be a judge, supreme court justice, assistant judge, justice of the peace, or an ordained or licensed clergyman. Nonresident clergy need to file for a permit from the county probate court where the marriage will take place. Vermont allows you to have a friend or a family member officiate at your wedding through the temporary officiant program. After paying the $100 fee and registering for the program, anyone meeting the requirements can be authorized to solemnize a specific wedding ceremony. Your fee for licensing will be $55, which includes a certified copy of the license.

Virginia

You will need a valid photo ID such as your driver's license, state or military ID, passport, and a certified copy of your birth certificate. If you have been previously married, some counties may ask for proof of divorce or death. There is no waiting period, and your license is valid for 30 days. You can marry your first cousin, but you cannot marry a partner of the same sex. Your officiant must be an ordained minister who can show proof of ordination, or a marriage commissioner, or an active or retired judge of either the circuit court or district court. Your fee will be $30.

Washington

You will need your Social Security number and most probably a picture ID. Your divorce must be final before you can apply for a license. There is a three-day waiting period, and your license is valid for 60 days. You cannot marry your first cousin, nor can you marry a partner of the same sex. However, the governor recently signed a law giving same-sex domestic partners all the rights of heterosexual couples except the word "marriage." Your officiant must be licensed or ordained clergy, or a justice of the peace. Your fee will vary from $42 to more than $62, depending on the county.

Washington, D.C.

You will need to show proof of age such as your driver's license, birth certificate, or passport. You will need to provide your Social Security number and date of birth, address, and home and work telephone numbers. If you were previously married, you will need a certified copy of the divorce decree or your deceased spouse's death certificate. There is a three-day waiting period from the time you apply to the time you pick up your license. The bureaucracy can take longer, so give yourselves five days just in case. You can marry your first cousin, and although you cannot marry a partner of the same sex in D.C., the district recognizes and gives full legal rights to marriages of same-sex partners from other states. Your officiant must be an ordained minister or justice of the peace. There is an application fee of $35 in cash for authorization to celebrate marriages in the District of Columbia. Your fee for licensing will be $35 to apply and $10 to obtain the certificate of marriage.

West Virginia

You will need a photo ID such as your driver's license, passport or state ID. You will need to know your parents' full names and your mother's maiden name, and the state in which they were born. Residents of West Virginia must apply for a license in their home county. If you were previously married, you must provide proof of divorce or death. You cannot marry your first cousin, nor can you marry a partner of the same sex. Your officiant must be an ordained minister authorized by the state of West Virginia. The court in each city and county has appointed persons who are eligible to perform civil weddings. Your fee will be $36 and up, depending on the county.

Wisconsin

You will need your driver's license with your current address or two pieces of mail with your current address, your Social Security number, and a certified copy of your birth certificate. You need to know your parents' full names including your mother's maiden name. You need to supply the date and place of your ceremony and the name, address and phone number of your officiant. If you are from out of state, you must apply in the county where the ceremony will take place. Residents apply in their home county. If you were previously married, you must have your divorce decree or the death certificate of your deceased spouse. You cannot remarry within six months of a divorce decree. There is a five-day waiting period exclusive of the day you apply. Your license is valid for 30 days. You cannot marry your first cousin, although some counties will make exceptions for those over 55. You cannot marry a partner of the same sex. Your officiant must be an ordained member of the clergy, a judge, a court commissioner, or certain religious appointees. You and your prospective spouse may officiate under established customs or rules of some religions. Your fee will be approximately $80, depending on the county.

Wyoming

You will need a driver's license or a certified birth certificate. You will need your social security number, your parents' full names including your mother's maiden name and their birthplaces. If you were previously married, you will need a certified copy of the divorce decree or a copy of your deceased spouse's death certificate. There is no waiting period, and your license is valid for one year. You cannot marry your first cousin, nor can you marry a partner of the same sex. Your officiant must be a judge, a supreme court justice, an assistant judge, a justice of the peace, or an ordained or licensed clergyman. Nonresident clergy need to file for a permit from the county probate court where the marriage will take place. Your fee will be $25.

INDEX

A

Affirmation 107, 148, 169
Alabama 185
Alaska 185
Albert of Saxe-Coburg 41
Alchemy (alchemical) 35, 47, 48, 146
Alexander, Robert 31
Alex and Richard 151
Alice and Hazel 89-92
Alyson and Jose 79-81
Alysha and Chris 85-92
Amelia and Ben 186
Angelo and Donna 152
Anjalee and Terry 83-85
Arizona 185
Arkansas 133, 185
Art 27, 28, 31, 36, 81, 141
Ashbery, John 158
Australia 10, 11, 27, 139, 142, 157, 174
The Art of Marriage 182

B

Baal Shem Tov 171
Backyard wedding 139, 142
Barnum, P.T. 43
Ben and Amelia 86
Benedetti, Kathleen 12, 102, 207
Bergman, Marilyn and Alan 112, 115, 207
Berlin, Irving 65, 207
Berns, David 47
Bhagavad Gita 25, 159
Bill and Keri 32-35
Binding 47, 51, 80, 86, 97, 127, 140, 148
Blessings 10, 17, 36, 63, 64, 74, 75, 77, 79,
    83, 84, 97, 110, 111, 128, 132, 144,
    150, 152

    Anonymous 176
    Apache 79, 158, 170
    Bradstreet 174
    Brennan 174
    Colossians 179
    Dante Aligheri 177
    Ebrecht 175, 207
    Ecclesiastes 177
    Flannery 169
    Four Directions 183
    Gibran 181
    Hindu 181
    I Ching 171
    Irish 170
    Kuan Tso Chang 172
    Marlowe 172
    Marti 175
    Muslim 180
    Petersen 182
    Song of Solomon 81, 83, 179
    St. Francis 178
    Twain 182
    Voltaire 172
    Whitman 173

Bowers 65, 80, 140, 144
Breath 46-47, 52, 88, 146, 148
Bradstreet, Anne 174
Brennan, Christopher 174
Browning, Elizabeth Barrett 2, 101, 159
Buddha 133
Buddhist questions 13, 14
Buddhist 13, 23
Burns, Robert 160
Butch and Sundance 150

C

California 186
Celebrant USA Institute and Foundation 11

Ceremonies
    Alex and Richard 151
    Alice and Hazel 89-92
    Alysha and Chris 85-86
    Alyson and Jose 79-81
    Angelo and Donna 152
    Ben and Amelia 86
    Chei and David 112-125
    Chris and Leah 97-99
    Gretchen and John 151
    John and Lee 69-70
    Joni and Jim 62-64
    Keri and Bill 32-35
    Kristina and Daniel 13-14, 23-24

Lisa and Eric 14, 22-23, 70-72
Maki and Ed 14-15, 20-21
Marc and Nancy 15, 17-18
Norlyn and Ed 19, 64, 65-66
Rosemarie and Ron 77
Sandy and PJ 97-11
Scott and Wallace 93-97
Stephanie and Michael 15, 16-17
Tammy and Jeff 66-68
Ted and Pam 61-62
Todd and Michele 72-74

Celebrating as a new beginning 9
Ceremonial Structure 17, 28
Ceremonies and Celebrations 157
Check to Cheek 65, 207
Chei and David 112-125
Children 15, 17, 18, 19, 23, 30, 32, 33, 34, 47,
    72, 77, 79, 80, 85, 86, 87, 88, 89, 90, 103,
    106, 108, 109, 112, 113, 114, 115, 116, 117,
    120, 123, 127, 128, 132, 133, 140, 141, 152,
    170, 177, 185
Chris and Alysha 85-86
Chris and Leah 97-99
Chupah 140, 150
Cinderella 30, 64, 113, 119
Civil Celebrant 10, 11, 12, 27, 37, 48, 72, 99,
    127, 155, 157, 177
Civil Union 89-91, 97-98, 133, 193, 194
Colorado 186
Connecticut 187
Cookies 106, 109-110
Council of Trent 42
Croft, Roy 154, 161
cummings, ee 63, 163

D

Dante, Aligheri 177
David and Chei 112-125
Daniel and Kristina 13-14, 23-24
DeBeers Mining 43-44
Defense of Marriage Act 133, 184
DeGeneris, Ellen 98
Delaware 187
Disney, Walt 41, 113
Divorce 10, 14, 15, 18, 22, 23, 27, 30, 62,
    64, 76, 77, 86, 102, 128, 129, 132, 133,
    185-200
Do It Yourself 153
Donna and Angelo 152
Dr. Seuss 67-68, 152

E

Ebrecht, Joyce 175
Ed and Maki 14-15, 20-21
Ed and Norlyn 19, 64, 65-66
Eliach, Yaffa 29
Elliot, George 171
Eric and Lisa 14-16, 22-23

F

Faith 2, 10, 15, 21, 22, 27, 33, 36, 49, 51, 98,
    99, 101, 107, 110, 128, 129, 150, 159, 176
Father 5, 16, 29, 32, 35, 43, 46, 69, 71, 74, 77,
    79, 85, 86, 95, 98, 103, 117, 118, 119, 122,
    123, 155
Feast of Life 94
Fire/flames 40, 46, 47, 49, 60, 61, 63, 85, 112,
    139, 145, 150, 172, 179
Fisher, Kathleen Benedetti 103
Flannery, Maureen Tolman 169
Flemming, Nancy Anne 45
Florida 187
Flowers 11, 32, 60, 62, 80, 84, 86, 87, 106,
    108, 112, 115, 138, 139, 140, 143, 144, 154,
    156, 173, 179, 182

Folktales
    It Was Enough 112
    Silver Tree, Gold Tree 130-131
    Stephanie's Parable 16
    The Lost Prince 71
    The Parable of the Water Bearer 31
    The Skywoman's Basket 134-135
    The Uninvited Guest 76
    Tiger's Whiskers 9-10

Food 9, 11, 14, 20, 60, 76, 95, 112, 140, 142,
    147, 156, 167
Fulghum, Robert 50, 54, 59, 160, 161

G

Garden Weddings 48, 61, 62, 80, 130, 131, 138-139, 140, 141, 142, 143, 152, 166
Georgia 188
Geretty, Francis 43
Gibran, Kahil 181
God 88
Grandchildren 89, 106, 109, 123
Gretchen and John 151
Guests 11, 17, 20, 30, 36, 40, 44, 46, 48, 51, 60, 61, 67, 70, 72, 73, 76, 79, 80, 83, 85, 94, 97, 107, 110, 112, 113, 114, 118, 136, 137, 139, 140, 141, 142, 144-50, 171, 175

H

Hasidic Tales of the Holocaust 29
Haiku Ceremony 149
Hamlish, Marvin 112, 207
Hawaii 30, 97, 188
Hazel and Alice 89-91
Heritage Foundation 127
Herrick, Robert 171
Hermes Trismegistus 35
Hindu Satapadi (7 steps) 181

I

Idaho 188
Illinois 188
Indiana 189
Invitations 21, 98, 147
Iowa 189

J

Jewish
  Ketubah(signing) 81
  Procession, bride and groom 4, 44, 45, 46, 48, 61, 72, 79, 80, 81, 83, 92, 106, 141, 145, 150, 152, 153, 154, 155, 168
  Chupah 65, 80, 140, 150

Joni and Jim 62-64
Jose and Alyson 79-81
Journey 2, 9, 10, 14, 16, 19, 39, 63, 64, 67, 68, 72, 74, 83, 85, 94, 102, 112, 116, 122, 132, 134, 151
Jumping Over the Pit 29

K

Kansas 189
Keller, Helen 34
Kempis, Thomas à 49, 161
Kentucky 189
Keri and Bill 32-35
Kisees 30, 52, 66, 72, 92, 96, 111, 130, 148, 154, 165, 171
Kristina and Daniel 13-14
Kwan Tao-Sheng 172

L

L'Chaim 114
Lawson, Jonathan 73, 207
Lear, Edmund 164
Lee and John 69-70
Life Magazine 47
Limmerick 157
Lisa and Eric 14-16, 22-23
Living Stage 31
Louisiana 133, 190

M

Maine 190
Maki and Ed 14, 15, 20-21
Marc and Nancy 15, 17-18
Marlow, Christopher 172
Marriage Law 26, 27, 86, 89, 90, 93, 98, 99, 133, 184-199
Marriage Variations in 21st Century 133
Marti, Jose 11, 117, 149, 175
Mary of Teck 42
Maryland 190
Massachusetts 191
Matthew 22 99
Menus 141-142
Messinger, Dally III 11, 12, 27, 157
Michael and Stephanie 15, 16-17
Michele and Todd 72-74
Michigan 191
Minnesota 191
Miss America 45
Mississippi 192
Missouri 192
Montana 192
Montclair 11
Mother 5, 19, 20, 22, 32, 69, 70, 74, 77, 79, 83, 84, 85, 95, 96, 98, 99, 104, 113, 116, 117, 118, 119, 122, 127, 131, 137, 152, 155, 187, 190, 191, 192, 193, 198, 199, 200
Murphey, Lionel 10, 11
Muslim 133, 150, 180
Music 14, 24, 28, 29, 36, 40, 45, 46, 74, 80, 95, 96, 108, 109, 111, 112, 119, 125, 137, 139, 141, 144, 145, 153, 181, 207

N

Name of God 88
Names, pronouncement 51, 168
Nancy and Marc 15, 17-18
Nebraska 193
Neruda, Pablo 70
Nevada 193
New Hampshire 193
New Jersey 194
New Mexico 194
New York 194
Norlyn and Ed 14-19, 64, 65-66
North Carolina 195
North Dakota 195

O

O'Neill, Edmund 34
Officiant 10, 14, 17, 27, 28, 31, 35, 36, 38, 45, 46, 48, 51, 80, 81, 86, 112, 144, 146, 147, 151, 155-156, 171, 184, 185-200
Officiant, choosing 112, 144, 146, 147, 151, 155-156
Ohio 195
Oklahoma 195
Orchids 31, 84, 85, 109, 143, 171
Ordinary Miracles 75, 113, 115, 207
Oregon 195

P

Pam and Ted 61-62
Parents 5, 15, 23, 45, 46, 47, 62, 67, 76, 77, 79, 80, 81, 85, 89, 91, 98, 112, 113, 117, 118, 119, 125, 140, 153, 184-200
Pennsylvania 196
Personal Happiness 14, 41, 77
Petersen, Wilfred 182

Poetry Titles
  Anonymous Limerick 157
  A Poem About How to Be A Husband, Purple Ronnie 37
  A Poem About Love, Purple Ronnie 38
  Beach Chairs, Ebrecht, Joyce 175
  Because She Would Ask, Bradstreet, Anne 174
  Bhagavad Gita 25, 159
  Give Me A Kiss, Herrick, Robert 171
  Had I The Heavens' Embroidered Cloth, Yeats, W.B. 167
  How Do I Love Thee? Browning, Elizabeth Barrett 159
  i carry your heart with me, cummings, ee 63, 163
  I Love You, Roy Croft 154, 161
  Intentionality, Flannery, Maureen, Tolman 169
  La Vita Nuova, Dante, Alighieri 177

  from Leaves of Grass, Whitman, Walt
  We Will Sail Pathless and Wild Seas 39, 173
  The Day When I Arose At Dawn 167

Love Is Born, Marti, Jose 111, 117, 149,
    175
Love's Philosophy, Shelley, Percy
    Bysshe 165
My Luve Is Like A Red Red Rose, Burns,
    Robert 160
No, I'll Not Take The Half, Yevtushenko,
    Yevegny 64
Ode To A Box Of Tea, Neruda, Pablo 70
Owl and The Pussycat, Lear, Edmund 164
Passionate Shepherd, Marlow,
    Christopher 172
Rivers And Mountains, Ashbery,
    John 158
Song of Solomon 83, 179
Sonnet 116, Shakespeare, William 166
Unending Love, Tagore,
    Rabindranath 129
With These Rings, Fisher, Kathleen
    Benedetti 103
You And I Have So Much Love, Kwan
    Tao-Sheng 172
You Have Become Mine, Hindu Satapadi
    (7 steps) 181

Porter, Cole 112, 113, 114, 207
Prince George of York 42
Procession 40, 44, 45, 46, 48, 61, 72, 79, 80,
    81, 83, 92, 106, 141, 145, 150, 152, 154,
    155, 168
Pronouncement 154, 168
Purple Ronnie 37-38, 207

R

Rajasthan 40, 181
Recommitment 101-126, 101, 102, 106, 108,
    112, 113, 114, 126

Readings
    A Marriage, Twain, Mark 87, 182
    Adam Bede, Elliot, George 171
    All I Really Need to Know I Learned in
        Kindergarten, Fulghum, Robert 59,
        161
    Apache Wedding Blessing 79, 158, 170
    Baal Shem Tov 171
    Because She Would Ask Me Why I Loved
        Her, Brennan, Christopher 174

Blessing of the Four Directions 84, 183
Book of Psalms 166
Corinthians 13 49
Ecclesiastes 49:12 177
From Beginning to End, Fulghum,
    Robert 50, 160
I Ching 171
Matthew 22 99
May All That You Are 97, 109, 183
On Love (Thomas à Kempis) 49, 161
Seven Blessings (Jewish) 177
Song of Songs 51:2 166
St. Francis's Blessing 178
St. Patrick's Blessing 170
Story of Ruth 180
The Art of Marriage, Petersen,
    Wilfred 182
The Prophet, Gibran, Kahil 181
The Verb To Love, Sloane, Pearl 156
True Love 86
Voltaire 172

RENT 207
Rhode Island 196
Ribbons 140
Ribbons 40, 43, 138, 140, 18
Richard and Alex 151
Rings 51, 51, 74, 89, 91, 93, 94, 96, 103,
    110-111, 125, 149, 207
Ritual 10, 11, 14, 16, 19, 20, 21, 24, 25, 27,
    26-39, 28, 35, 36, 38, 40, 41, 42, 43, 46, 48,
    49, 50, 51, 52, 60, 61, 64, 67, 72, 77, 79, 80,
    83, 86, 91, 93, 94, 97, 99, 107, 112, 114,
    126, 132, 138, 144, 146, 149, 151, 152, 153,
    154, 155, 156, 169, 170, 171
Rosemary and Ron 77

S

Same Sex Marriage 89-100, 133, 193, 194
Sandy and PJ 97-111
Sarma, Pat and Gail 11
Scott and Wallace 93-97
Secular Sprirituality 27
Shakespeare, William 166
Siddhartha 133
Signing 46, 86
Silver Tree/Gold Tree 130-131
Skywoman's Basket 134-135
Sloane, Pearl 156

Song Lyrics
    Cheek To Cheek 65
    I Have The Moon In My Bed 68
    Let's Fall In Love 114
    Ordinary Miracles 115
    Seasons Of Love 73
    You're The Top 115
Song of Solomon 83, 179
Soul 10, 34, 35, 63, 65, 69, 114, 115, 116, 120,
    128, 129, 130, 131, 132, 133, 144, 159, 163,
    168, 171, 181, 183
South Carolina 196
South Dakota 197
Spanish Language 81, 82, 116, 207
State Regulations 186-200
Stephanie and Michael 15, 16-17
Step-parents 77, 79
Sublimity 28, 72, 139, 145
Symbols 10, 30, 35, 60, 63, 69, 131, 144, 152

T

Table Settings 143
Tagore, Rabinndranath 129
Tammy and Jeff 66-68
Tea Ceremony 69
Tennessee 197
Terry and Anjalee 83-85
Texas 197
Thelma and Louise 150
Time 25, 102, 106, 153
Tom Thumb 43
Top Hat 65, 76
Transformation 2, 46, 48, 64, 96, 98, 102, 113,
    128, 130, 131, 141, 146, 150, 152, 154, 168
Trees 20, 61, 103, 104, 139, 151, 166
True Love 86
Twain, Mark 87, 182

U

Unending Love 129
Unity Candle 33, 46, 47, 63, 85
Utah 198

V

Vanderbilt, Consuelo 42
Variations in Marriage 133
Vermont 198
Victoria, Queen of England 41, 42, 45, 66,
Victorian 2, 41, 51, 66, 138, 168
Virginia 198
Voltaire 172

W

Wallace and Scott 93-97
Warren, Lavinia 43
Washington State 199
Washington, DC 199
Water Ceremony 83-84
Wedding Cake 138
Wedding Costs 11, 136
West Virginia 199
Whitman, Walt 39, 167, 173
Wisconsin 200
With These Rings 103
Words, Power of 16, 19, 31, 134, 146
Wyoming 200

Y

You're The Top 115, 207

Z

Zen 13, 23
Zoroastrians 46

PERMISSIONS

RIVERS AND MOUNTAINS, by John Ashbery. Copyright © 1962, 1966, by John Ashbery. Reprinted by permission of George Borchardt, Inc., on behalf of the author.

"With These Rings" by KATHLEEN BENEDETTI-FISHER.
Used by permission of the author.

Ordinary Miracles by Marilyn and Alan Bergman, Marvin Hamlisch
©1994 Red Bullet Music and Threesome Music Company. All Rights Administered by SONY/ATV Music Publishing LLC, 8 Music Square W, Nashville, TN, 37203. All Rights Reserved. Used By Permission.

"Cheek to Cheek" by Irving Berlin
© Copyright 1935 by Irving Berlin
© Copywright renewed. International Copyright Secured.
All Rights Reserved. Reprinted By Permission.

"I carry your heart with me(I carry it in" Copyright 1952,© 1980, 1991 by the Trustees fro the E.E. Cummings Trust, from COMPLETE POEMS: 1904-1962 by E.E. Cummings, edited by George J. Firmage. Used by permission of Liveright Publishing Corporation.

"Beach Chairs" by JOYCE (LAYTON) EBRECHT. Used by permission of the author.

Hasidic Tales Of The Holocaust by Eliach p3-4 © 1982 by Yaffa Eliach. By permission of Oxford University Press, Inc.

"Intentionality" by MAUREEN TOLMAN FLANNERY. Used by permission of the author.

ALL I REALLY NEED TO KNOW I LEARNED IN KINDERGARTEN by Robert L. Fulghum, copyright © 1986, 1988 by Robert Flughum. Used by permission of Villard Books, a division of Random House.

FROM BEGINNING TO END by Robert Fulghum, copyright © 1995 by Robert Fulghum. Used by permission of Villard Books, a division of Random House.

I HAVE THE MOON IN MY BED from MUSHROOM MUSIC, Words and Music by PAUL KELLY AND THE MESSENGERS

Seasons Of Love
From RENT
Words and Music by Jonathan Larson
Copyright© 1996 Finster & Lucy Msic LTD. CO.
All Rights Controlled and Administered by UNIVERSAL MUSIC CORP.
All Rights Reserved Used by Permission

"Ode To A Box Of Tea" from ODES TO COMMON by Pablo Naruda. Copyright © 1994 by Pablo Neruda and Fundacion Pablo Neruda (Odes in Spanish) Copyright © 1994 by Ken Krabbenhoft (Odes in English): Copyright © 1994 by Ferris Cook (Illustrations and Compilation). By permission of LITTLE, BROWN & COMPANY.

YOU'RE THE TOP (from "Anything Goes")
Words and Music by Cole Porter
© 1934 (Renewed) WB MUSIC CORP.
All Rights Reserved

LET'S DO IT (LET"S FALL IN LOVE) (from "Paris")
Words and Music by COLE PORTER
@1928 (Renewed) WB Music CORP
All Rights Reserved

"Purple Ronnie Love Poems" by Purple Ronnie, copyright © PRNA 2009. Used by permission of COOLABI.

"Unending Love" from RABINDRANATH TAGORE: SELECTED POEMS translated by William Radice (Penquin, 1985) Copyright © William Radice, 1985. Used by permission of Penquin Group (UK).

"No, I'll Not Take the Half" from Early Poems by Yevegny Yevtushenko, trans. And ed. by George Reavey, (Marion Boyars, 1989)